A TWIST OF THE WRIST
VOLUME II

A TWIST OF THE WRIST VOLUME II

THE BASICS OF
HIGH-PERFORMANCE
MOTORCYCLE RIDING

BY: KEITH CODE

CODE BREAK

Acknowledgements

Editor
John Ulrich

Design and Illustration
Joe Spencer Design

Assistance
Judy Code – Life Support
Donny Greene – Wiley Coyote

Inspiration
Marcel Duchamp – Words into motion
L. Ron Hubbard – "Key to Life™" course
Doug Chandler – #1 his way

Photography
John Flory, pages xv, 92
Patrick Gosling, pages 7, 15, 58, 75, 102
Dennis Scully, page 104
Brian J. Nelson, back cover
Lance Holst, pages xiii, 47, 112
Fran Kuhn, pages 22, 72
Maurice Bula, pages 14, 32, 59, 84, 101, 11⁴
Rich Chenet, page 9
Courtesy: Motorcyclist Magazine
Courtesy: Roadracing World

Copyright 1993 Keith Code
Library of Congress Cataloging-in-Publication Data
(revised for vol.2)
Code, Keith
A twist of the wrist.
Vol. 2 has imprint: Glendale, CA, Code Break
Contents: v. 1. The motorcycle roadracers handbook — v. 2. The basics of
high-performance riding.
1. Motorcycle racing — Handbook, manuals, etc.
Doug Chandler. II, Title.
CV 1060.C53   796.7'502'02   82-73771
ISBN: 0-9650450-2-1

Printed in the United States of America

Distributed by:
California Superbike School, Inc.
PO Box 9294
Glendale, CA 91226
800 530-3350

Warning: Riding and racing motorcycles is both fascinating and exhilarating, partially
due to the fact that you risk injury or death by your own or other's errors and actions
while doing it. This book is not intended to nor does it claim to remove any of the
potential dangers of riding motorcycles. It is in fact possible that reading and applying
this material could lead to increased exposure to any or all of the potential dangers of
riding motorcycles. This book contains a written account of observations made by the
author and others: based on their personal experience. The author and others
acknowledge the fact that they have ignored or were possibly unaware of dangers to
themselves and may have been in the position to observe these things only because
they knew it was dangerous and even desired that danger: and accept no responsibility
for your individual application of the contents of this book which might result in any
harm, injury or property damage to yourself or others.

Always wear protective riding gear and observe local speed laws. Consult your state
approved licensing program for proper riding procedures.

Foreword

The information in this book got me where I am now in roadracing. From what I can see, the whole idea of this book is for you to apply it to your riding, like I do. A lot of the things might look too fancy for the street but mostly they apply to both street and track.

Some information that people tell you just gives you a headache but Keith's ideas teach you how to think for yourself. Over the seven years we worked together we didn't have it all written down like this, so it should be easier for you.

No one likes to think that panic reactions can take them over but you need to look at it as a barrier to be overcome. Once you see these mental blocks written here you'll recognize them because they happen all the time and that's where your mistakes will come from.

In lots of ways I'm just now getting comfortable with different parts of riding and I've been doing it for over twenty years. Don't be in a hurry, I've seen guys in a hurry and they don't make it. You've got to get these ideas firm in your mind and then get comfortable with them in your own style, no matter how long it takes; because if you don't get these ideas you won't get any farther.

Doug Chandler

Contents

Margin Notes and Comments by Doug Chandler

Chapter-end Comments by Donny Greene

Author's Note

The 10 years since the publication of the first **TWIST** book have been exciting ones for motorcyclists. That volume was my first attempt to create a **technology*** of riding: I knew there was one, it was simply a question of finding it. And TWIST has been well received worldwide, mainly because it provided riders with a format for discovery and thinking about their riding; it was a useful first step. But **TWIST OF THE WRIST VOLUME II** contains more **real riding technology** than **TWIST I** and it addresses the source of our classic rider problems. Let me tell you what I mean by **real riding technology**.

Technology Versus Tips

I want to outline the different **categories of information** you might receive about riding your bike. There are four; remember them. Each piece of info that comes your way will fall into one of these categories.

Destructive Advice:

"You don't know how fast you can go until you crash."

"Wait till the other guy brakes and count to two."

Friendly Advice:

"Keep the rubber side down."

"Be smooth."

Useful Tips:

"Go wide around that bump."

"Try this section in the next taller gear."

Real technology:

"You always use a later turn-entry point for a decreasing-radius turn*."

"Going off and on the throttle in turns affects suspension compliance, reduces traction and makes the bike run wide."

Real Solutions

True **technology** has broad application and regularly resolves riding problems. It contains a basic understanding of **what** the rider is trying to do and forms a constructive bond between the rider and the machine's dynamic* requirements. Counter-steering is a perfect example. (See Chapter 12 for a description of counter-steering).

Practically everyone learns how to ride without any understanding of counter-steering, but the moment it is fully comprehended and applied, it opens the door to vast amounts of improvement in every possible situation that requires steering the bike. Counter-steering perfectly matches what the rider wants and needs with what the machine wants and needs. That's what I call **technology**. Do you see the difference between that and useful tips or friendly advice?

I'm not saying there isn't a place for tips and advice, because there is—when they demonstrate an understanding of honest technology in practical application. Then a tip or piece of advice becomes a useful tool. But I've listened to many sincere words of advice on riding, most of which were worthless.

Discovery

To the enthusiast rider, motorcycles are all about discovery and challenge. That hasn't changed in the over 100 years motorcycles have existed, and that won't change as long as there are motorcycles. Riders still regard their time in the saddle as a quality experience: There is adventure in every curve of the road, every freeway ride, every twist of the wrist. And unlike so many things in life which become boring once they are understood, just the opposite occurs when a rider begins to grasp and apply the technology of riding. The technology of riding opens the doors of discovery instead of closing them.

Accepted Technology

A German philosopher named Schopenhauer once stated, "All truth passes through three stages. First, it is ridiculed*. Second, it is violently opposed. Third, it is accepted as being self-evident*." **Riding technology** has undergone this same process.

Going through a set of esses on my 200cc Ducati in 1960, I discovered counter-steering. It scared me. It didn't make any sense and I never mentioned it to anyone until the 1970s for fear of being told I was nuts. Counter-steering didn't become a piece of **understood technology** until 1973, during an international conference on motorcycle safety held in San Francisco. There, Dr. Harry Hurt and a group of Honda researchers each presented technical papers documenting how counter-steering worked and how its conscious use could benefit motorcycle riders by making it easier to avoid collisions.

The counter-steering researchers had opened the door to riding improvement for everyone. But I also remember the upsets and arguments created when I tried to explain counter-steering to a disbelieving veteran with 20 years of riding experience.

Similarly, it was a long-held belief that using the front brake was out-and-out dangerous. This "advice" was given freely, especially to new riders, usually by salesmen at motorcycle dealerships! In some circles you could almost get into a fist fight about it. Now, of course, "everyone knows" the front brake has the lion's share of stopping power.

In 1976 I claimed that racers could improve by simply understanding more about riding. I wrote up several short bulletins, mainly useful tips, which seemed to work for myself and others. When it leaked out that I was having my students look up words in a dictionary and demonstrate these written ideas with drawings or small objects on a table, I was openly criticized by many of my fellow racers. But these students began making big improvements in their riding. In fact, they averaged 7.0 seconds a lap faster. But it wasn't until a brave young journalist and racer named John Ulrich took the program in 1977 and publicized his findings that it got even a nod of recognition from the racing community. The rest, as they say, is history.

In this volume are a few more key pieces to the puzzle.

Keith Code

PS: You'll note that key words are indicated by an asterisk when they first appear in this book. Knowing the true meaning of each key word as it is used in the text is essential to understanding. The definition of each key word appears at the end of the section in which it first appears.

Definitions

Technology: The application of knowledge* for practical ends.

Knowledge: Acquaintance with facts, truths or principles, as from study or investigation.

Decreasing-radius turn: A turn that tightens up as you go through it.

Dynamic: Force as it relates to motion.

Ridiculed: Made fun of.

Self-evident: Plain or clear in itself without additional proof or demonstration.

Motorcycle Technology vs. Rider Improvement

Since my first motorcycle (1957), machine evolution has been staggering. Bikes are lighter, faster and handle better; tires are stickier and suspension systems more compliant*. But after 13 years and over 20,000 students as headmaster at the California Superbike School, I still see the same riding problems in the 1990's which existed in the 1970's and 1980's. In fact, even though our Superbike School equipment is over 20 mph faster than it was 13 years ago, student lap times have improved only 1.0 to 2.0 seconds on the average. This fact, when compared to the racer's typical lap-time improvement of 8.0 to 10 seconds for comparable equipment, brings up a number of interesting questions **and** answers to the subject of high-speed riding.

Machine technology has moved ahead of most riders' ability.

What's the Stop?

What stops riders from being able to use this clearly improved bike technology? (Current tire grip alone is probably worth 3.0 seconds of improvement). What are the common barriers which hold them back? (There must be something if so many are uncomfortable at speed). Can more education in riding techniques* alone overcome the barriers? (The 1990s rider already knows more than did his early 1980s counterpart). Does more track time handle it? (My experience says it is not guaranteed by more saddle time). Does the desire to go fast put one rider over another in his quest for speed? (No. I've had potentially* talented riders, who wanted nothing more in the world than to race, not make it). Seems pretty grim* for the would-be racer, doesn't it? (Just hold on a moment).

75 Percent Perfect

I call it the Mental Speed Block.

What I **have** discovered is that 95 percent of my students reach unexpected new levels of confidence after only half a day of classroom plus track training, and half of them can be coached to a high degree of technical skill in two days: **but only if they ride at about 75 percent of their limit.** What happens after 75 percent? Everyone agrees, in some fashion, **survival* reactions*** (commonly known as fear) are the ever-present barrier to reaching their goals. Once the standard riding techniques are understood, this is the one button (also called panic) that nearly everyone pushes, **at their own personal limit.** This agreed-upon fact is what ruins* riders' attempts to reach the goals they have envisioned* for themselves. It ruins self-respect, confidence and trust in oneself in the process.

*The **last** thing to try is charging the turns.*

Survival reactions not only consume your $10 worth of attention, they are the cause of your riding errors.

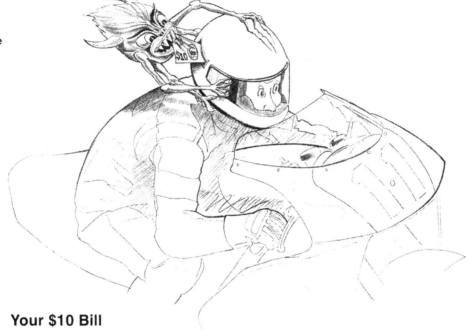

Your $10 Bill

Start with easy braking and get the line to prepare for faster entries. Try to get comfortable with corner speed then get the entry speed up.

Something like the Carousel at Sears Point with all those bumps can get your attention and you want to use the brakes but it will lock up too easy. You spend too much on them.

The idea (from the original Twist Of The Wrist) that everyone has just so much **attention*** (like money) to spend on the actions of riding has not changed. If you start out with $10 in your pocket and spend it all, you are broke and having no money causes its own kind of **panic.** Having **no attention** left to perform the needed actions while riding (like target fixing on some object you don't want to hit and then hitting it because that is where **all your attention was spent**) always creates some panic. **All riders, at one time or another, have overspent their "$10 worth of attention" and survival-reactions, like fear and panic, are the direct results.** In this book we figure out how to cheat (or raise the limit of) and defeat (beat) **the major source of riding problems**, your **panic button.** Spend your **attention** wisely and push **the button** lightly.

This book is a great tool for helping you to understand what can push the "panic button". Learning and practice will allow you to "push back" these barriers and open up more room for having fun at any speed.

D.G.

Definitions

Compliant: Yielding to request or demand.

Techniques: The body of specialized procedures and methods used in any specific field.

Potentially: Possibly but not yet actually.

Grim: Stern and forbidding in aspect or nature.

Survival: The act or fact of surviving, especially under adverse or unusual circumstances.

Reactions: Actions in response to some influence, event, etc.

Ruin: Demolish, destroy, damage.

Attention: 1. Focused awareness. 2. Directing the senses toward something known or not known.

Envisioned: Picture mentally.

Donny Greene at work. With 5 National 250 GP titles to his credit and six years as guest instructor for the California Superbike School, Donny's comments are a welcome addition to the text.

A TWIST OF THE WRIST VOLUME II

CHAPTER ONE

The Enemy

"Survival" Reactions

Survival reactions (SRs) come from our instinct to avoid injury but often cause the opposite. There are seven classic SRs riders should know about.

Survival reactions are truly automatic because they originate* from a source we do not consciously monitor*. For example, we do not have to monitor our eye blinks (to protect the eyes) when something unexpected happens. However, the reliability of these reactions is subject to question when one either freezes (another **reaction**) or **reacts** inappropriately*. **Survival reactions** are not totally healthy. I watched a rider crash in turn nine at Riverside Raceway (a four-lane, 40-foot-wide, banked turn with a steel boiler plate wall on the outside) on the bottom or inside lane (10 feet from the grass). The rider then ran completely across three lanes of track, to the outside of the turn, to a 5.0-foot wall, "to safety," on a hot (open for practice or racing) track.

Survival Devices

Devices* and mechanisms* have been designed to reduce injuries related to these reactions. A workable example is the friction-reducing metal or plastic skids on glove palms which minimize sprains and breaks resulting from riders extending their hands to "cushion" the impact of crashing—one of the classic **survival reactions**. Anti-lock brakes provide a high-tech solution to excessive, **survival reactive** braking. To a degree, sticky tires provide a cushion for overbraking and sudden extreme lean angles.

Survival Errors

Each of the common, garden-variety **survival reactions** most of us have can either cause or contribute to crashing. On the less dramatic* but very important side, they are the source of 100 percent of all rider errors. They do, in fact, **ruin** your riding. Let's look. On a motorcycle, **survival reactions** have specific* results. Each carries with it enough force and command* value* to change the rider's mind **and** control actions. Take, for example, rolling on/off the throttle while cornering. My survey of over 8000 riders concluded that **not one** of them ever intended to roll on/off; that 100 percent of them intended to roll it on, throughout the turn, as their basic plan. Something changed their minds. **Rolling off the throttle is survival reaction (sr) number 1.** Survey shows it to be the front line of defense when any circumstance* triggers a **SR**. The standard* **SR triggers** are:

"In too fast."

"Going too wide."

"Too steep lean angle."

"Concerned about traction."

Bumps, traffic and others are secondary sources of unneeded throttle roll-off. That riders most often realize the roll-off **was not necessary**, right after doing it, is also further proof it was an automatic **SR**. Ever happen to you?

Survival Reactions

The enemy is tough but limited in number:

1. Roll-off the gas.

2. Tighten on bars.

3. Narrowed and frantically hunting* field of view.

4. Fixed attention (on something).

5. Steering in the direction of the fixed attention.

6. No steering (frozen) or ineffective (not quick enough or too early) steering.

7. Braking errors (both over- and under-braking).

Survival reactions (SRs) usually affect the arms first. Your arms control: steering, braking, throttle and influence handling.

Everyone has had all of the above happen to them. Are they automatic? Take tightening on the bars as another example. Do you command your arms to tighten up, or do you find they have done it on their own? Do you choose to have your attention narrow and target fix? Did you over-brake on purpose?

Whether for a real or an imagined reason, anything that triggers one of the above **survival reactions (SRs)** is an attempt to reduce or avoid injury. **None of them work in harmony with machine technology or rider control.** In the following chapters we will see how to defeat them.

It's great that these things have finally been pinpointed and instead of just being the adverse affect of them everyone can now see what they are. Instead of just continuing from one **SR** to another, perhaps now riders can use this information to nip them in the bud, before they become too dramatic. After racing for 13 years I hate to admit that I even have them but it's like a little devil on my shoulder, they keep popping up. Now you can head them off at the pass.

D.G.

Definitions

Originate: To arise from some origin or source.

Monitor: To oversee, supervise.

Inappropriately: In a manner not proper or suitable.

Devices: Something made, usually for a particular working purpose.

Mechanism: An assembly of moving parts performing a complete functional motion.

Dramatic: Of or like the drama; theatrical, vivid, striking.

Specific: Definite, particular or precise.

Command: The act of ordering, authority.

Value: The worth of a thing, importance.

Circumstance: A condition, detail or part, with respect to time, place or manner which accompanies an event.

Standard: Usual, common or customary.

Hunting: The act of searching for, seeking.

Imagined: To form a mental image of (something not actually present).

Notes

CHAPTER 2

Throttle Control

Rule Number One

Can a **survival reaction** like on-and-off the throttle be educated and practiced out? What does the bike do in response to this common error? What motorcycle **design* features*** are violated by **survival reaction**-generated* throttle errors? Are there **rules** and **procedures*** for combatting them? What are the **positive** survival and skill **improvements** in store for the rider who beats them? This and the next four chapters explain.

Understanding the Gas

Throttle control is a very precise subject with its own rules and standards*. The **techniques of throttle control** are directly descended* from motorcycle engineering* specifications* and allow your bike to perform up to the level for which it was designed. **Throttle control techniques** list-out like a manual of requirements any modern-day bike **demands** of its rider. Understanding your bike's specifications of performance is step one in overcoming the throttle control Survival Reactions (**SRs**) which detract from your riding.

Traction Specifications

Real acceleration is the exit of the turn, the end of it.

When we talk about cornering we are talking about traction as the rider's main concern. To determine an ideal* scene for traction, machine-wise, we start by simply measuring the contact patches* of the tires to discover what the basic distribution* of loads should be while cornering. Roughly speaking, those measurements* show that 40 percent of the total load should be up front, 60 percent at the rear. Bikes set up for racing and real GP machines carry more rear rubber, changing the useable load bias* (possibly to as much as 70 percent on the rear) to favor hard acceleration coming off turns. Each bike's exact ideal weight distribution may vary a bit from the basic 40/60 percent rule. **The rider's task is to match the exact load specs of his machine with expert use of the throttle.** How do you do that?

The distribution of cornering loads follows your tire's contact patch size—about 40% front to 60% rear. You adjust the tire load with the throttle. (shown smaller than actual)

Light Touch

Considering that most machines in a static* or constant speed situation have a 50/50 weight distribution (+ or − 5.0 percent) front-to-rear, we begin to calculate the guidelines* of correct acceleration through a turn. By the numbers, we want to transfer* 10 to 20 percent of the weight rearwards, using the throttle. Technically, this is 0.1 to 0.2 G* of acceleration. Simply put, it's the force generated by a smooth fifth-gear roll-on in the 4000 to 6000 rpm range on pretty much anything over 600cc. **That's not much acceleration—but it does the job.**

It seems riders often have difficulty sorting out this small amount of traction-maintaining-throttle through turns, instead trying for more dramatic acceleration. This is most easily seen in the common error of being too "greedy" with the throttle at roll-on, which will make the bike run wide or slide and lead to a roll-off.

You can start the "drive" too early by getting the front light and run wide. That will hurt your time for the straight.

In every corner open the gas as soon as possible; light acceleration thru the middle.

Rule Number One

Once the throttle is cracked* on, it is rolled open evenly, smoothly, and constantly* throughout the remainder of the turn.

At the point where the **correct** transfer of weight is achieved by the rider (10 to 20 percent rearward) by using the throttle, any big changes in that weight distribution **reduce available* traction**. Once the bike is fully leaned into a turn, changes in tire load, either evenly (both wheels, most easily done in a crested road situation) or alternately (front to back, back to front, from throttle on/throttle off) must then either underweight or overweight the ideal load for that particular tire/bike combination.

It's not worth trying to get to the speed you "think" you should have had: you'll only make it worse trying to get it.

Never play with the throttle through the corner.

No one is likely to chop the throttle in World GP racing.

Riding Skill

Each guy feels something different. His set up and line might not work for you. You have to start by getting comfortable on the machine.

The rider's special skill in applying Rule Number One is in his understanding and sensing of the bike's requirements and delivering them with his "by the book" use of the rule. **Riders do not improve their bikes, they simply help their bikes to work correctly.**

No chopping on and off before you've made the corner, it loads the front. Work on getting it cracked open first.

Obviously, **any** major hitches, hesitations or throttle on/throttle off actions cause less than the ideal scene to be achieved* and herein* lies the problem with **SR** #1: It destabilizes* the bike's traction picture*, **instantly**. The faster you're going, the more dramatic the effect. Getting to and keeping a 40/60 percent weight balance is your basic **throttle goal. Throttle rule number one combats SR #1.**

Lost Ground

Whether your bike slides or not from throttle on/throttle off isn't all that can happen. In a medium-speed turn (40 to 80 mph), each throttle on/off/on will cost you at least 0.10-second in lap time (in terms of distance, over one bike-length) even if you are very good, and more if you aren't very good. In higher-speed turns, the same throttle error will cost you more because the effects of wind-drag* are substantial* in slowing a bike at the higher speeds.

Entering a little slow isn't so bad. You can get on the gas earlier. You don't lose as much time as you think you would if you take advantage of it by getting it picked-up and exit quicker.

Survival Training

As a **survival reaction**, on/off the gas ranks first. Street riding makes the consequences* of it seem mild and forgivable. In this sense, street riders train themselves to do it wrongly by simply allowing **SR** #1 to occur. On the other hand, the basic rule of throttle control can **almost always** be applied, at **any speed**, because it holds true for **99 percent of all turns** and **traction conditions**. (The exceptions are very rare, like a long downhill, decreasing-radius*, off-camber and bumpy-in-the-middle turn. But even here you shouldn't really roll off the throttle; you just stop rolling on for a moment).

Take a surprise slippery road situation, in a curve, as an example. Coming up to it and snapping off the gas will transfer 70 to 80 percent of the bike's weight onto the front wheel, which is designed to carry only 35 to 40 percent while cornering. Staying on the gas is no guarantee the bike won't go down but you have to ask yourself this question: Are the chances of making it through the slippery corner improved or not improved by keeping the gas at least cracked on? Are the chances improved or aren't they? Consider the extreme error of applying the front brake while leaned over and in slippery stuff, an error almost certain to result in a crash: That's the direction you're going when you roll-off the throttle!

Going off the gas while sliding the rear would create an enormous handling problem!

Gas It

Is the bike more stable or less stable when it has the correct amount of weight on each tire? The old racing rule of "When in doubt, gas it!" does most certainly have some validity*.

An extreme example of this happened to Doug Chandler at Sears Point Raceway in 1989, while he led the 750cc Supersport race on dry pavement. His rear tire was so "cooked" that it began to slide going into the turns simply from being off the gas. (Another potential hazard of on/off the gas in high-load-cornering situations.)

One lap he put down a strip of rubber at least 30 feet long as the back "came around" (slid) and the steering went **all** the way to stop. Staying off the throttle would have led to, without question, a massive highside*. Of course, being the talented dirt tracker he is, Chandler turned on the gas, the rear tire spun and the bike wobbled as it straightened out but he stayed on board and in the lead. On the gas was the **only** solution. What would **you** have done?

Questions

What is **SR** #1?

What is the definition of good, standard throttle control?

Does it agree or disagree with machine design?

How often does your right wrist roll off the throttle without permission?

Since every bike has a different set-up it is extremely important to have a good feel for what the bike is doing in the corners. The information in this section will allow you to fine tune your weight distribution. There is a thin line on throttle control where you always want to be hard on the gas, I'm guilty of it too, but championships are won when it's done by the book. This **SR**, on and off the gas, not only costs time but in 250 racing it costs positions.

D.G.

Definitions

Design: Invention of the forms, parts or details of something according to a plan.

Feature: A prominent part or characteristic.

Generated: Produced, brought into existence.

Procedures: A course of action. A way of performing or effecting something.

Standard: Something considered as a basis for comparison. An approved model.

Descended: Derived; come down from a source.

Engineering: The science and art of planning, constructing and managing structures of various kinds.

Specification: A detailed and exact description of materials, dimensions and workmanship for something to be built, installed or manufactured.

Demand: To call for as necessary. An urgent or pressing requirement.

Detract: To take away something desirable: Diminish.

Ideal scene: An idea of something in its perfect state.

Contact patch: The actual foot print of the tire where it contacts the road surface.

Distribution: The division of something into portions.

Bias: An inclination or preference.

Static: Showing little or no change.

Guideline: Any guide or indication of a future course of action.

Transfer: To shift from one position to another.

G: A unit of force equal to the gravity exerted on a body at rest.

Cracked-on: Opened a slight bit into operation.

Constantly: In an unchanging manner.

Remainder: Anything left over; a remnant.

Available: Ready for use or service.

Achieved: Reached successfully.

Proportion: A portion or part in relation to the whole.

Here-in: In this.

Destabilize: To disturb the smooth functioning of.

Picture: A situation or set of circumstances.

Wind-drag: The resistance of the wind against the body or bike at speed.

Substantial: Ample or considerable.

Consequence: The result or outcome of something occurring earlier.

Decreasing-radius turn: A turn that tightens up as you go through it.

Off-camber: When the inside of the road is higher than the outside in a turn.

Validity: Being well grounded: Soundness.

Highside: The act or situation in which the rider is thrown over the top side of the bike, towards the outside of a turn.

Notes

Throttle Control

Suspension and Traction

Mechanically* speaking, we depend on the suspension* for our traction. What can a rider do to make the best of his bike's suspension? Is it necessary to have a $15,000 set of GP-quality Ohlins forks and shock? Do you already have the tools for good handling? What is "good handling" anyway?

Use most of the front end travel and about 75% of the rear. But, if you get it too soft in front, the back end will come around.

At rest, a motorcycle is handling great. No wiggles, wobbles, bounces, shakes or slides: It is stable*. A perfect suspension and rider combination would keep the tires on the ground with the bike stable, in all riding conditions. **Good handling = predictable* traction.** That is **all** it means.

There's nothing quite like an **unexpected** loss of traction (slide) or the **threat** of loss of traction (**unpredictable traction**, like a good wiggle or head shake), to stimulate **survival responses** in most riders. And just as tire size has given us a good starting point for figuring machine demands, a quick look at the suspension parts helps us determine **how the rider can put the suspension to best use with standard throttle control.**

Suspension Range

Good suspension depends on both the **hardware** (shock, forks, weight of parts) and its **position** on the bike, (head angle, fork offset, engine location) for stability. Throttle control has a huge effect on both.

There's no substitute for a correctly adjusted suspension but it's the rider's job to keep it in range with standard *throttle control*.

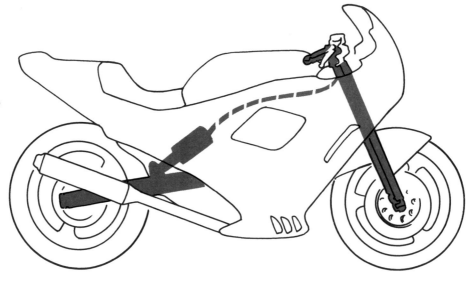

Shocks and forks produce the best road holding/traction mid-stroke (in approximately the center third of total travel). Fully compressed ("bottomed") suspension is rough and "topped out" (fully extended) suspension similarly lacks good response to road conditions. Hard braking and hard acceleration offer perfect examples. When the rider is hard on the brakes, the front-end feels heavy and reacts sluggishly over any rough pavement because it is unable to react to surface changes. (Note: This is also a major reason why the front wheel will lock under braking. The wheel cannot follow the road surface because the front forks won't move up and down quickly enough or won't move up and down at all). When the rider is hard on the gas, a light front end tends to shake and tank-slap. In the middle third of the suspension stroke (or travel), you get good feedback and optimum* response to the asphalt.

In long turns the front will stay down if you increase the rebound damping but too much will make it pack up: it won't return from each bump.

If you have too soft or too hard a spring it can make it chatter on the gas.

Riding Limits

Suspension limits how we can ride motorcycles. We must try to keep the suspension in its most useable range, as much as possible, and allow the bike to work for us. The basic rule of **standard throttle control** does precisely that. Here again, the on-gas/off-gas riding technique used by most riders forces the suspension to solve* huge weight transfers (front-to-rear) instead of reacting to the pavement: Yet suspension design does not allow it to do both jobs well at the same time.

It's simple: Off gas turns quicker because it steepens the front. On gas increases fork angle and steers heavier.

Suspension Changes

Suspension characteristics* can be adjusted to suit the rider and road surface by changing the damping* rate, spring pressure and weight bias, front to rear. **You never eliminate basic suspension problems**, you only make adjustments to suit conditions. In racing, adjustments can make **what** happens at one lap-time/speed-range reoccur in a higher range; in that case, you've simply moved **where** it happens so you can go a bit quicker.

Front-end chatter* is a good example of how tricky suspension can be. With some bikes, chatter will appear at slower lap times, making the rider think he has reached the suspension's limits; more speed makes the chatter go away but it appears again when even faster lap times produce still higher cornering loads. A streetbike is typically set-up for more general conditions, usually for the rider's favorite type of turns.

The Rider's Suspension Adjustment

The handiest suspension adjustment you have is throttle position. For every bike, within basic design limitations, throttle application* gives you enormous control of how much weight is on either wheel while cornering. Obviously, **throttle on too much** transfers weight **onto** the rear wheel, **off** the front wheel. In the case of a 600-pound bike-and-rider combined weight, you have at your fingertips a control (the throttle) which will effectively move 150 pounds forward or aft with **no more** than a few millimeters of movement! **Throttle control is the key to suspension set-up.**

Suspension Gas

Riders can chase a suspension problem forever, make dozens of adjustments and never get anywhere. Nothing will work if the rider runs into a corner hard, off the gas, waits until late in the turn and then, using hard acceleration, tries to over-ride the ideal 10-20 percent weight transfer to the rear tire. That approach **never allows the suspension to work in its best range*.** This is especially true in simple, medium-speed, 90-degree turns taking only 2.0 or 3.0 seconds total time to enter and exit. The same riders who favor the approach described above can often be seen "testing" suspension in the pits, bouncing the forks up and down and pushing on the seats. They're paying the most attention to the part of the suspension stroke they rarely use on the track.

In 1989, John Kocinski slaughtered the 250cc class here in America, setting track records **no one could touch** for years. He told me at the time that the team had made no significant suspension changes in five races! He had made them with the throttle.

Rear Suspension and Gas

Most riders don't understand this simple fact: The harder they twist the gas, the less compliant the rear suspension is and and the more the rear end tries to **rise**. Most riders believe that the back of the bike goes down when they accelerate. It doesn't. (To test this, put the front wheel of your bike up against a wall and begin to engage the clutch with the transmission in gear. The rear end will come up.)

Again, the standard rule of throttle control: **once the throttle is cracked on, it is rolled on smoothly, evenly, and constantly throughout the remainder of the turn.** As luck would have it, this basic rule works perfectly with the interesting fact of motorcycle dynamics described above. In a turn, the 40/60-percent weight loading that produces the best traction also puts the suspension in its most useable and workable range.

"Whacking" the throttle on stiffens the rear suspension and reduces traction. That's a problem for most of us. Yet the best riders have figured out a way to completely reverse the situation and use it to their advantage. In the case of a 500cc GP bike, (or even a good Superbike), when the power starts to come on and the suspension stiffens, the tire tends to spin because traction is reduced. What do the best riders do? They let the tire start to spin for the drive out of the turn. The suspension actually becomes more compliant right when the tire begins to spin, because the reduced traction relieves some of the load. It's the same principle taken to a new level.

Most guys chop it but the solution to sliding is picking-up the bike with the gas steady.

Fancy riding like that looks good but the basics still apply. The **earlier** the throttle is cracked open and smoothly rolled on, the **less** "desperate" acceleration you need to build speed coming off the turn, and the more compliant the rear suspension will be. That produces the most predictable traction. This applies to any kind of riding, not just racing.

Slide Insurance

Throttle rule Number One, the smooth roll-on, has other distinct* advantages you should know about, especially during a rear-end slide. Provided you weren't already too greedy with the throttle, your best insurance against more sliding or a highside is simply to stop rolling on the gas. The bike slows gradually, rather than quickly (as it would from chopping the throttle), and comes back into alignment* smoothly. Here again, **SR** #1 is your major obstacle.

(Obviously, tire condition, lean angle, suspension and the rider can be big factors* in this but don't take my word for it, watch the best racers get through little slides. Does the throttle go off or do you hear the engine continue to rev at a constant or higher pitch?)

Why?

Look at machine design. If the back end is "coming around" and you chop the throttle, you have a big weight transfer off the rear wheel. That weight transfer can promote more sliding of the rear tire or overload the front tire, possibly enough to make it slide.

Off-Gas Problems

Trying to slow down with too much speed or too much lean will start it sliding.

So, off-the-gas also has its downside. Off-the-gas makes the rear suspension compress along with the front suspension. If you come off the gas mid-turn, you lose cornering ground-clearance* at both ends, instantly. Here is another **SR #1** example: Say the rider drags some part of his bike, then shuts off the gas in surprise or alarm; instantly the bike is dragging even more, maybe even lifting one or both wheels off the pavement. **SR #1** has struck again.

What is the basic rule of throttle control?

Once the throttle is cracked on, it is rolled on evenly, smoothly, and constantly throughout the remainder of the turn. (Say it to yourself 1000 or 2000 times).

Most standard suspension components can be set up to work adequately, even on the track, without the need for expensive parts. Besides that, it feels really good to beat the guys with the trick parts. Good parts or not, grabbing a handful won't help you to go fast, that's a dangerous way to make up for low corner speed. The bike and the tires will **not** like it. Once you have the throttle control rule firmly understood and practiced and you can get the rear wheel spinning with a smooth roll-on, your bike will handle again.

D.G.

Definitions

Mechanically: Having to do with machinery.

Suspension: The system of springs and dampers that protects the chassis from shocks transmitted through the wheels.

Stable: Resistant to sudden change: Steady, reliable.

Predictable: Being what was expected. Capable of being foretold.

Standard: Authorized or approved.

Optimum: Most favorable or desirable.

Solving: Finding the answer to.

Characteristics: Distinguishing features or qualities: Traits.

Damping: A restraining or discouraging force or factor.

Chatter: The vibration from the tires caused by the rapid gripping and releasing of traction.

Application: The act of applying or using.

Range: The scope of the operation of something.

Distinct: Unquestionable: Definite.

Alignment: Arrangement or position in a straight line.

Factor: One of a number of things that contribute to a result.

Ground clearance: The distance between the motorcycle chassis parts and the ground.

Notes

CHAPTER 4

Throttle Control

Everyman's Ideal Line

*Setting up a bike to both hold your line and scrub off speed in slow and medium turns **and** still work in the fast stuff is one of the most difficult things to do.*

It's simple: Crack it on — let it settle — come into it.

Everyone has a "line" through every turn he ever rides. It is the path traveled, a description of real estate used to negotiate* the turn: That's the definition. But, how do you determine* the best line? If you find a good line, how do you hold it? What could hold you back from choosing and using a good line?

The whole subject of **lines** is far simpler than I first imagined, and it follows the basic rule of **throttle control**: In fact, it is almost identical*. **The line that allows the throttle to be applied, exactly by the rule, is an ideal line.** (The line that does not allow the throttle to be applied, exactly by the rule, is not an ideal line.)

No matter which line you use, good *throttle control* makes it work.

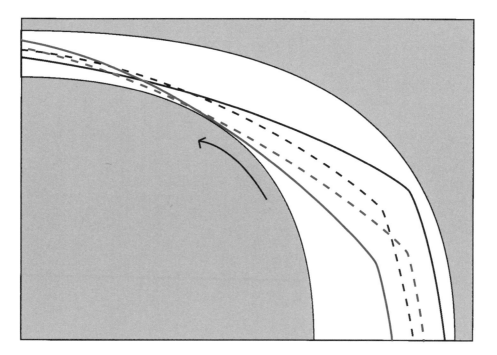

Different Strokes

I don't mean to mislead you. The "everyman's ideal line" does not exist, and it never will. Different lines are the rider's own personal way of seeing and doing his job: A concatenation* of his strong and weak points, dos and can't dos and machine limitations, and, of course, his **SR** threshold*.

Also, pavement variations (bumps, ripples, patches, etc.) can affect traction adversely* and prompt the rider to change his line. To deal with a pavement problem, you (1) change your suspension, (2) change your line or (3) ignore the problem and continue. A top rider will come up with a combination solution of all three. Number three is the hardest to achieve because it means overcoming your **SR responses** to the track conditions.

On the racing circuits, riders routinely* complain about the track being "rougher than last year." At first, **any changes** they note are bad ones. Yet normally, by the end of the weekend, everyone is going faster than they did the year before!

Find the Line

Each time you back off the throttle or slow your basic throttle roll-on through a turn, it costs time and stability. Your approach to the turn determines whether this happens or not. Decreasing radius (DR) turns are the classic example (see diagram). Taking a standard approach to the first radius **always** forces you to back-off the gas in mid turn. That's not an ideal line because it immediately violates the **throttle rule**.

Let's not confuse a double-apex turn with a DR. In a double-apex turn (see diagram) you may well roll off the gas to get the bike turned between the two parts of the corner. This allows you to **fully** and **correctly** control the throttle on the exit* of the second part of the corner and not be "stuck" with holding the gas steady. In fact, "stuck on the gas" is one of the primary indicators that you have a "bad line." Of course! It violates the throttle rule.

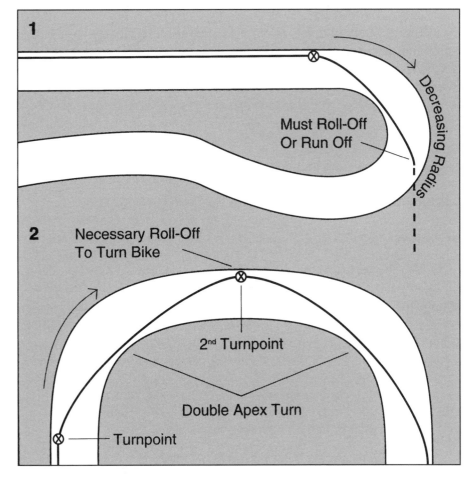

1

Must Roll-Off
Or Run Off

Decreasing Radius

2 Necessary Roll-Off
To Turn Bike

2nd Turnpoint

Double Apex Turn

Turnpoint

There is a big difference between a Decreasing Radius turn and a double apex turn. *Throttle control is the key to both.*

Line Follows Gas

Line follows gas, or, ride for the throttle: a good line allows standard use of the throttle. There is no other definition of a good line.

Stuck On the Gas

If you aren't rolling-on throttle in a turn, you're slowing down. Indeed, you can be rolling on but too slowly and still lose mph! Most riders think that just cracking the gas on makes the bike accelerate. Not true. Try it. Go into a turn on your streetbike, just crack the throttle and watch the speedo. (Use a safe place to try this, like a racetrack). If you've got the bike leaned over much at all, you'll see the speedometer reading drop. You have to be rolling the throttle on just to hold a constant speed (50/50 weight distribution), let alone to accelerate hard enough to reach the ideal 40/60 weight transfer. (You haven't forgotten this from Chapter 2, have you?)

Hold It

You can't say it too much: Gradually increase the throttle without getting out of it.

Under what conditions will your bike hold a constant* line through a turn? Off-the-gas transfers weight forward, tending* to make the bike stand up and run wide. On-the-gas too much does the same thing, widens the line. (Note: if you think your bike goes to the inside of the turn when you come off the gas, you're unconsciously steering it to the inside. Tire profiles and suspension settings may have an effect on this as well)

The only reliable way to hold a constant line through any turn is with standard 40/60 throttle control. This is another one of those machine requirements*: It is an **ideal scene** for the bike; it is how you achieve stability in a turn with respect* to your line's radius*. Just ask yourself. Is it good to have a predictable line? Is it a plus to know where the bike is going, up ahead in the turn? Do you notice small changes in line? Most important: Do changes in line fire up your **survival reactions**?

Isn't it interesting that "in too fast" or "going too wide" **trigger SR #1** (roll-off)? In turns, **SR #1** puts the bike precisely where you don't want it, doing precisely what you don't want it to do (running wide).

Exception

There is an exception* to the throttle control rule: Wide-open, top-gear turns. Turn One at Brainerd International Raceway is a perfect example. You come into it after **one mile** of straightaway. On a current 600cc or 750cc production or a 250cc GP bike, the turn is taken with the throttle wide-open. What can you do? You can't roll on the throttle because it's already full on. What happens if you're halfway or two-thirds of the way through a wide-open turn and you roll off/on? You go wide, **right now**, the bike bounces around and is **not** stable. (This is one of the most challenging and fun turns in America. On a 250cc GP bike it is taken at 13,000 in sixth gear, or about 159 mph at the entrance).

An interesting side note: How would you gear your bike for Turn One at Brainerd? Would you have it reach peak rpm at the end of the straight, a normal gearing goal? Not on a 600, 750 or 250. Once you lean the bike over it will pick up about 500 more rpm because you're running on a part of the tire which has a smaller diameter*, effectively lowering the gear ratio. So if you geared for the straightaway you'd be bouncing off the rev limiter at the entrance to the corner and the bike would not be near 40/60 weight distribution. The solution is to reach the 40/60 goal with the gearing instead of the throttle. If you geared the bike to run 500 or so rpm lower than normal at the end of the straight, the engine will continue to pull once you're in the turn and the bike will hold the line perfectly.

Fine Point?

The above is, at first glance, a very fine point of riding but it actually contains a practical lesson for every turn. Remember that leaning into a corner effectively lowers the gear ratio. If you downshift too many times and put the engine in too high an rpm range at the turn entry point, the moment you lean over you could be stuck on the rev limiter instead of pulling through the corner smoothly. The bike will, of course, slow down from the cornering forces and wind drag in any turn and at Brainerd you have to downshift at the exit of Turn One to keep the revs up. The point is not to be stuck on the rev limiter mid-turn.

Along these same lines, you may glance at the tach (while still leaned over) coming off a long sweeper onto a straight, see the tach needle at the redline, and think it's time to upshift: It isn't, because as you stand-it-up* onto the larger-diameter center of the tire, the revs will then go down. If you upshift too early (especially on a 250cc GP bike) the bike won't pull strongly and you'll have to wait for the engine to build rpm.

Tire diameter varies greatly from straight-up to leaned-over. This has a big affect on engine RPM in turns.

An ultra-fine point is gearing a 500cc GP bike so that it runs into the rev limiter, on purpose, at the turn **exit**. In this case, the rider is spinning the tire and allows the rev limiter to cut in so the wheelspin does not become excessive and wind up highsiding him. The power tapers off smoothly and the rider can leave it on the rev limiter for a moment with no ill effects. The only drawback is having to shift before the bike is totally vertical. How's that for precision bike set-up and riding?

21

Other Exceptions

There are a few other specific turns that do not follow the rule mainly because of bumps and/or mid-turn (off) camber changes and radius changes, and they are downhill. The carousels at Sears Point and Road America are perfect examples. You do have to stop the throttle action (not roll-off) for a moment or two or you will simply be going too fast and too wide at the exit where the roll-on is most important.

Power Line

The power characteristics of your bike and the suspension settings have much to do with your line. On a 500cc GP bike, you may drop some cornering speed to use the acceleration. On a 125cc GP bike, you can't sacrifice cornering speed for anything. If its suspension makes the bike a little slow to turn, you'll have to wait longer to stand it up and be easy with the gas mid-turn to avoid running wide.

The farther you lean it over, the longer you will be "stuck" with the throttle.

Starting the real acceleration too early will make you have to re-adjust your turn and lose time.

Perhaps you've noticed some riders standing the bike up rather quickly towards turn-end whereas others allow the bike to arc* through and come up gradually*. Slow steering might be the answer as to why. So might the fact that the rider is a bit greedy with the gas, earlier in the turn, and has to keep the bike leaned over to stay on the track. He may just like to do it that way. (Of course, the quicker the bike is stood up, the less resistance* you have from the cornering forces and the faster you accelerate).

The End

Let's clear something up. Where does a turn end? Each turn has an exact point where it ends. That point is different for each rider and each bike. Definition: Where you can do anything with the gas you want to, where you are brave again, where your attention is free from the turn, where you are sure you can do it better next time; that's the end.

The important point: **there is a choice in lines but they all follow the throttle rule.**

The track surface is the same for everyone on a race course, the best riders just adapt quicker. With problem areas you have to come up with a plan or a solution so you don't become stuck in anything; mainly you just handle the **SRs** and that covers it. I get a good mental picture of myself in every turn to get a starting point, then go out and do it. I Use the same mental image pictures to get an idea of what the bike should be doing as well as what I should be doing as an ideal for the turn. There is a time to think about it and a time to do it.

D.G.

Definitions

Negotiate: To successfully move through, around or over a given terrain.

Determine: Decide or settle: To conclude after reasoning or observation.

Identical: Exactly equal and alike.

Concatenation: Being linked or connected in a series: A chain.

Threshold: The point at which a stimulus begins to produce an effect.

Adversely: In a contrary or unfavorable manner.

Routinely: Regularly; a usual procedure.

Exit: The end of a turn.

Constant: Not changing or varying: Uniform; regular.

Tending: Being inclined to do something.

Requirement: A thing demanded. That which is necessary.

Respect: With regard to, in relation to.

Radius: A straight line extending from the center of a circle to the edge. The curve of a turn.

Exception: An instance or case not conforming to the general rule.

Diameter: The width of a cylindrical object.

Stand-it-up: To bring a bike from a leaned-over position to an upright one.

Arc: To move in a curve.

Gradually: Changing by small degree; little by little.

Resistance: A force that tends to oppose or retard motion.

CHAPTER 5

Throttle Control

Get It On

If good throttle control is responsible for good cornering control, (i.e., suspension in best range, tires delivering optimum traction, line predictable, etc.), when would you like it to start? In what part of the turn should you have all these good things happening? Exactly **when** do you **get it on?**

Street Lazy

Street riders generally wait until about two-thirds of the way through a turn before they roll the throttle on. Under normal low-speed or urban* traffic situations a motorcycle does not seem to mind if you coast through turns. Most new riders take to this coasting technique like a duck to water because it does not trigger the "in too fast" or "going too wide" **SR** responses. Under more spirited cornering conditions, all the positive results of good, standard throttle control are reversed while off the gas, decelerating.

Off-Gas Results

1. Weight is forward, overloading the front tire and underloading the rear, reducing available traction.

2. Suspension is out of its ideal range, causing the bike to over-react to the pavement.

3. Steering response quickens, adding to any twitchy tendencies.

4. The bike wants to wander outward, not holding a line.

5. Cornering ground clearance is reduced.

6. The bike slows.

When you get to the throttle determines **where** the bike is actually working. The earlier into a corner you get onto the gas the sooner you have the suspension in-range*, weight transferred and so on. The later into a corner you get onto the gas, the more likely you are to be gas "greedy" for the exit. (It's a term I learned at a Skip Barber car school, and I repeat it here because it describes this situation perfectly).

When do you "get it on"? When you want the bike to start working — as soon as possible.

When?

As soon as possible. You get the gas on at the earliest possible moment in a corner. This does not mean at the apex*, right before the apex or right after the apex or at any particular part of the turn, it means as soon as possible.

You judge how fast to enter a turn by getting to the point where the back comes around a little bit. But even then you want to get it lined up by getting the gas on.

How?

There are some additional guidelines. Normally, riders don't get back onto the throttle until after the steering is completed. This makes sense. During the steering process, it is very difficult to work back into the throttle smoothly enough to keep it from jerking the bike and upsetting it. To meet the throttle standard, steering is completed before you start to get it on.

In a turn and at speed, drive-line lash* is annoying; it upsets the bike. Rough or sudden movement of the throttle, from off to on, creates the same effect. The change in weight distribution from 70 front/ 30 rear (off the gas) to 40 front \60 rear (on the gas) is done as smoothly as possible to maintain stability and traction.

Steering and throttle are linked. Turning the front end into the turn and getting the back to come around can only be done on a few turns in the U.S. Like the old turn #2 at Loudon. You have to muscle the bike to do it and you've got to be leaned way over or it will counter-steer back up instead of biting and turning in.

Waiting too long for the bike to settle is wrong thinking. Getting the gas on early does not add problems, it solves them!

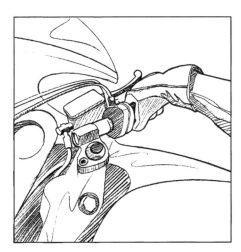 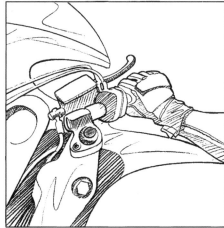

Throttle Plan

What keeps you from getting it on sooner than you now do? It can be as simple as (1) you never thought about it, or (2) it scares you. Getting the throttle cracked and rolling-on early and smoothly should be your basic plan, **at every turn**.

Overcoming the very strong **SR trigger**, which forces you to stay away from the gas, simply has to be handled and can be handled with practice. Perhaps it can be tamed with understanding.

If you don't lose traction going in, getting to 40/60 won't make it crash, it will make it handle.

Take another look at Off-Gas Results 1 through 6 above: You don't add new and unwanted forces by rolling-on, you reduce them all. **Your job is to reduce them as soon as possible.**

Throttle 1/10ths

In real time and space, each 0.1-second that you stay away from the gas is over one bikelength of distance in a 60 mph turn. In fact, it is 8.8 feet. (60 mph = 88 feet per second; 120 mph = 176 feet per second).

On a 500 you have to get it upright as soon as possible for the hard drive. One or two tenths late and it costs you half a second on the straight. You have to get them turned and pointed. Corner speed isn't as important as on most other bikes.

To put 0.1-second in even better perspective*, snap your fingers twice as fast as you can. That short time between the two snaps is 0.1 to 0.2-second! Now, how many of these precious little 1/10ths do you spend while waiting for the bike to settle or to get a fix on lean angle or speed or traction? It doesn't take much to burn up 0.5-second (two lazy snaps) and you're 44 feet down the road.

It doesn't mean you lost 0.5-second in lap time, it means you didn't have the bike working well over that length of track and there is a time loss as well.

100ths

Averaging 1.0 mph faster (60 mph vs. 59 mph) through one short turn (150 feet measured from straight-up going in, to straight-up coming out) gives you 3/100ths of a second improvement in lap time or puts you about 2.6 feet ahead of a competitor travelling 1.0 mph slower than you;

that's about 1/3 bike-length. On a nine-turn track (if all the turns were 60 mph), even if you could not gain one foot on him down the straights, you would be nearly 24 feet ahead by the end of the next lap; that's over three bike-lengths! In a long (1280-foot) turn at 120 mph vs. 121 mph, the difference in speed translates into 6/100ths of a second and 1-1/2 bikelengths. The reason behind the old racer's saying, "go fast in the fast turns," is obvious from these numbers. The reasoning in the other wisdom*, "don't try to make it up in slow turns," becomes clear as well. You'd have to go nearly 5.0 mph faster to make up that 1-1/2 bikelengths in a slow turn! Forget it!

Get It On

Each moment you hesitate* in cracking the gas and getting to 40/60 weight distribution reduces your average speed through the turn, lessens control and handling and increases lap times.

You always aim to get the bike pointed by mid-turn, that gives the most options with the throttle on the way out.

I try to get the throttle on just before max lean angle for the turn. This is how you get the bike to settle into the turn comfortable. The grip on the right is the fun regulator.

D.G.

Definitions

Urban: Of or dealing with a city or town.

In-range: In the operating scope of something.

Apex: The mid-point in a curve.

Lash: The amount of free-play in the chain, cush-drive and gears.

Perspective: The relationship of one aspect to another and the whole. A view.

Wisdom: A wise saying or teaching.

Hesitate: To wait to act because of fear or indecision.

CHAPTER 6

Throttle Control

The Force

Is too much **force*** fuel for the panic machine? Too much speed, too much acceleration, too much braking, too much cornering force and so on? Too little or the right amount of these **forces** never overwhelmed* anyone. If you could control them at a higher level than you now do, would your riding be better? Controlling the **forces** on a motorcycle prevents you from being confused and overwhelmed by your **survival reactions**.

A Little Too Much Force

Sometimes you can just get overloaded and frozen, then you windup off the outside of the track.

Confusion can result from either too many forces **or** too much. A fascinating* experiment was conducted with people at a university in which a small amount of heat (not enough to burn), and a small amount of cold (not excessive), were added to an electrical current (not enough to shock), and when touched to the skin produced the sensation of **intense pain**. Riding involves various forces that act on you; none of them are difficult to handle individually but how about when they come together, like in the experiment?

Clearly, riders are able to handle the amount of speed that allows them to stay on top of their **survival responses** and still keep track of the other forces of riding—without becoming overwhelmed. That's why most riders have at least fair riding at 75 percent of their ability and big errors at 80 percent and above. A very important example follows.

The various *forces* created while riding are both the fun and terror of it. We use these forces to gauge ourselves.

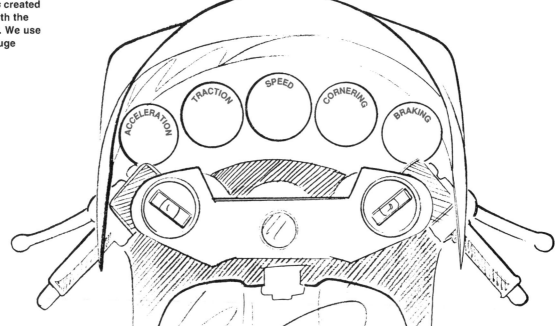

Charging

In high-speed-entry turns, the most common error is **"charging"** — going in as far as possible with the gas wide open, then chopping the throttle hard and having to coast in or brake lightly to scrub-off the excess speed. Riders always give up **far too much speed** as a result of this style of riding. And since the largest gains in lap times are made in high-speed turns, charging becomes a huge **barrier** to lap-time improvement.

If you start slow and accelerate you might feel instability, front tuck or it just won't track but it could still work at the higher speeds; start slow.

Discharging

Here are the steps for lowering the voltage from this self-generated* **SR**:

1. Approach the turn at a speed you **know for sure** you can handle. Let's say this is a sixth-gear turn and the fast guys are going in wide open at 13,000 rpm. You start out 3000 or even 4000 rpm under that. You approach the turn at a constant throttle, at that rpm.

*The **last** thing to try is charging the turns.*

2. As you turn in, roll-on the gas to get the 40/60 weight transfer. Remember, this is at a non-threatening speed so rolling on should not produce any panic whatsoever or do anything except make the bike stable.

3. The next pass is done a few hundred rpm higher. Depending on the bike and gearing, each additional 1000 rpm produces roughly 10 to 15 mph in sixth gear. Every time you move up the scale 500 rpm, you raise your speed about 5.0 to 7.5 mph. Each 100 rpm is 1.0 to 1.5 mph.

4. Continue steps 1 through 3 until you reach your limit or the bike's limits. This gets the speed right and avoids the **SR's** triggered by **"charging."**

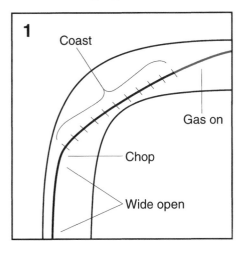
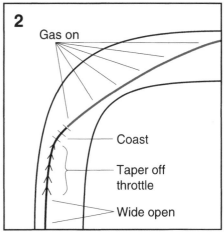

"Charging" turns makes you late coming back in the throttle (1). The calm, controlled approach may feel slower but usually it's much faster (2)

Recharge

For turns that really aren't wide open, the additional steps to this drill are:

Some guys think they have to be just quick but you have to be controlled.

1. Approach the turn wide open but start the roll-off **well before** you would if you were charging and make it a smooth, even roll-off.

2. Get the throttle cracked open and rolling-on right away. As above, if you are approaching it one step at a time, you will find the limits of this turn in the safest and most controlled way possible.

The "kink" at Road America, the carousel at Sears Point, Turn Nine at Laguna, the infield sweeper at Daytona, Turn Two at Willow, are more examples where this has worked. **In many cases the rider finds he never had to roll-off completely.** Or, he finds he rolls-off but only for an instant, just long enough to know where off is. Any idea of using the brakes is just a memory. **Another SR defeated by understanding throttle control and machine basics.**

Be Suspicious

In any turn (real braking turns excepted) where you are tempted to chop the throttle and/or use the brakes lightly, look at it with a suspicious* eye and see if good throttle control won't gain an even better result. Amping-up your **SRs** by **charging** may be exciting but not fast and charging doesn't agree with machine design.

Throttle control rule number two: in any fast-entry turn, calculate the roll-off as carefully as you would a roll-on.

Does this also agree with suspension design, weight transfer and traction?

Force Gauges

We use the various forces created by our machines in many ways; in fact, we gauge* most of what we do by them. Forces produced by braking, accelerating, cornering, etc. are the **real stuff** of riding. We come to depend* on some of them for information or feedback. However, as in the above examples of Charging turns, they can be deceptive*.

Sorting Out The Forces

Perhaps it is difficult to sort-out* the difference between the higher (around 1.0 G maximum) load of the braking and cornering forces from the much less pronounced acceleration (.1 to .2 G) required for optimum traction/suspension. Many riders have trouble with this point. **Throttle control produces the least of the forces encountered while cornering—when done correctly.** As your turn entry speeds come up and you get on the throttle earlier, you will begin to discover just how light a touch mid-turn throttle requires.

Emotionally*, shifting your senses from heavy braking and cornering to light acceleration loads may have some bearing on why it is difficult. After all, abandoning* a greater force for a lesser one, when you're trying to go fast, even sounds wrong. However, we are talking about machine requirements, not a rider's dreams of factory rides.

The Forces At Work

Any turn is full of important forces to monitor. There's deceleration from brake, engine and wind drag coming up to the turn; the force created

When the bike is tracking OK it's easier to sort out your speed. If it goes out of line or twitches from chopping it, you can't feel it as easy.

The majority of your senses going in are focused on speed. Once in the turn, you want to sense the bikes' feedback.

by turning the bike, the load from the tires "setting," then cornering (tire friction vs. centrifugal* force); then acceleration plus cornering and wind drag (in fast turns) through the middle and exit. Just as in the pain experiment, individually, none of them may be a problem, but two or more together can cause confusion.

Forces are something you deal with while riding. The standard techniques of throttle control put you in command over many of the forces, and one of the by-products is defeating the **SRs** that accompany those forces. In correctly using the throttle—to set entry speed—you are making it a little easier on yourself and on the bike.

Speed is the force that lights up our SRs quicker than anything: throttle control is the way to tame them.

At one track it took Keith 10 years to talk me into using the throttle correctly in the fast turn entries. Gently rolling off and back on at a similar rate can eliminate time consuming complications such as: shutting off the gas, grabbing the brake and just getting it cracked back on just right. Of course, all the riding time I have has helped sort out the different loads a rider feels on the bike but now I feel as though I can sort them equally and not have any one of them consume too much attention. Another simple but useful tool is knowing these different ways that the bike slows (The Forces at Work) each of them can be used individually or, sometimes, altogether.

D.G.

Definitions

Force: Strength or power exerted upon an object.

Overwhelm: To overcome completely as by physical or emotional force.

Fascinating: Having the power to capture interest and hold the attention.

Self-generated: Produced from within.

Suspicious: Believing something to be false, undesirable or bad.

Calculate: To determine by reasoning, common sense or experience: To figure out.

Gauge: To evaluate or judge.

Depend: To rely on.

Deceptive: Misleading; creating a false appearance.

Sort-out: To find the differences between one thing and another: To clarify.

Emotional: Of or relating to emotion; involving any of the feelings of joy, sorrow, fear, hate, etc.

Abandoning: Leaving or ceasing to operate or inhabit.

Centrifugal: Moving or directed outward from the center.

Centrifugal Force: The tendency of a body rotating about an axis to move outward.

SECTION 2

CHAPTER 7

Rider Input

Riders Create More Problems Than Motorcycles Are Designed To Handle.

Based on the amount of wiggling, squirming and overuse of controls most riders exhibit, the bike would, if it could, surely ask them to leave. Much like an uneducated passenger who tries to "correct" by counter-leaning* mid-corner, riders create instability on their own mounts.

Hanging-*On* can be as important as Hanging-*Off*. The awkward seating position is an attempt to find a stable place to hang on.

Rider Technology

As an example, most Novice Knee Draggers try to **hang off** and **steer** at the same moment. This is a big mistake as it only serves to make the bike wiggle at their turn-in point. One of the reasons the **hanging-off** riding style works so well is that your body is already in a low and stable position on the bike when you **flick** it into the corner. The correct technique is:

1. Get over into position well before the actual steering input, usually just before you roll off the gas and pull on the brakes.

2. Stabilize yourself for the braking but be comfortably seated so you will not have to make any additional body position changes throughout the entire turn.

3. Clamp onto the bike, just tight enough, with your outside leg or boot pressed to the bodywork or, in some cases, use the tank by pressing your knee against the side or your arm across the top of the tank, or do all of the above.

4. Apply steering pressure to the handlebars. You're in the turn!

Stability

In the esses*, where one turn immediately follows the other, you **time your steering** so it comes right after you settle to the seat. The mistake is trying to turn while you're moving from one side to the other side of the bike and aren't firmly and comfortably anchored to it. There's almost no way to completely eliminate quick-turn transition* wiggles but trying to steer while you're off the seat adds unnecessary input into the bars because they become your primary* pivot point.

In esses, you're always trying it quicker but start slower and smoother so you finally get to turning it when your weight hits the seat.

Trying to steer and hang off at the same time and trying to steer while moving from one side of the bike to the other are just two of the ways riders contribute* fuel for their **SR** fires and upset the bike in the process. The next four chapters explain how to remain in maximum control of your bike with the minimum amount of effort.

Don't just sit there like a lump on the seat, help the suspension, use your legs like an extra set of shocks.

D.G.

Definitions

Counter-leaning: The act of a passenger on a motorcycle leaning in the opposite direction from that of the rider.

Esses: Two or more turns in succession, generally capable of being taken at high-speed and laid out in an elongated "S" shape.

Transition: Movement or passage from one place, state, stage, etc. to another.

Primary: First: First in order of any series.

Contribute: To give (money, time, assistance, force, etc.) to a common supply, fund, effect, etc.

CHAPTER 8

Rider Input

Holding On

Have you ever noticed your **forearms pump-up** while riding? Do your **hands become tired** during or after spirited corner-carving sessions? These are two of the main indicators (there are many more) telling you **something is wrong**. What are the indicators saying? How you hold onto the bike is quite an art all in itself. In fact, it is actually a separate technology with its own rules (Wouldn't you know it?), its areas* of agreement and disagreement with machine technology and, naturally, **SRs** that can ruin your riding time.

You have to build confidence in the bike, your first "instinct" is to tighten up.

Do you command your arms to tense-up or do they do it automatically*? Do you need further proof this is a **survival reaction**? Try this. Take a series of turns at-speed* and stiffen-up your body on purpose as you ride through the turns; really hold the bike and bars tight. For most riders, it's the only way to discover exactly what's happening. Generally, riders don't notice their pumped-up arms until they slow down. Is this automatic?

Too tight on the bars is *survival reaction #2.*

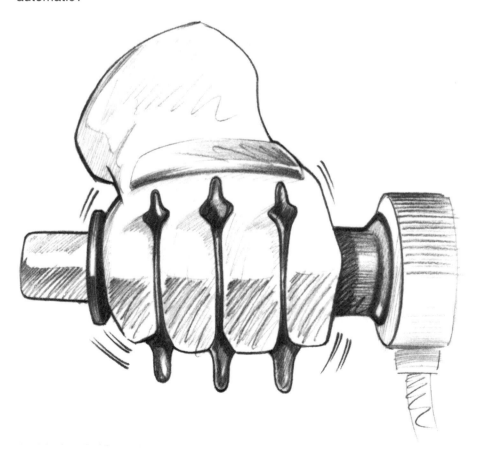

Survival Reaction #2

Again, by survey of over 8000 riders, the overwhelming choice for runner-up in the "unwanted riding conditions" class is: **too tight on the bars.** The same triggers that cause roll-off/roll-on also fire up this **unconscious action**. And **yes**, it is the sole* reason for the message your arms and hands are sending home to you. The message is: Please send oxygen, we are overworked and starving.

My first inclination* is to simply say, "relax on the bike," but, because we're dealing with **SR's**, it's not that easy. If there was a way to simply hot-wire (bypass) these reactions, I'd tell you, but there isn't. But we can handle them, using education as our primary tool. So let's get smart about **holding on**.

Machine Demands

Depending on road surface conditions, speed, tires and suspension **your bike will head-shake**, a little or a lot, with some combination of these influences*. **Any bike will do it.** What most riders fail to realize* is that this shake is a **necessary** part of the bike's suspension system*. This system has two stages we can see right away, (1) the tire, and (2) the shock and forks. The tire handles some of the road's imperfections because it's rubber and flexes*. When it reaches its limit of flex, the shock and forks take over to stabilize the bike. What happens when these two systems fail to handle the situation? **The forks move, side-to-side.** They are the next thing that can move and they do. Why do they move?

When (1) and (2) above have reached their limits the immediate result is weight changes to the tires. Heavy/light, light/heavy. A spread-out contact patch* (when weighting is heavy) forces the forks to turn inwards. When weighting lightens up, the forks seek to return to the centered or neutral position, to track* for the lean angle you have. The fork doesn't quite stop right at the perfect tracking position, it goes slightly past it. By this time the tire has hit at least one more surface imperfection and is going through the light/heavy phase again, spreading the contact patch and turning it inwards, then out and so on and so on. That's what shakes the head.

Stop Shaking

No one is strong enough to stop this from happening. In fact, **if you did stop it, the bike would instantly wobble violently and be totally out of control.** The good news is that if your bike is basically tight (steering head bearings not excessively worn, forks and shock not sticking, etc.) the head-shake stays up front and does not transfer to the rest of the bike. The bad news is that these head shakes are transferred, back **through the rider**, after SR #2 has kicked in.

Riding a dirt bike in deep sand offers a dazzling* example of this principle*. Hold tight and the bike feels totally unstable and ready to crash; loosen up and it goes straight, even though the front end is working back-and-forth. Riding over rain grooves cut in the highway can offer a milder sample of the same principle.

When you try to "force" the bike to go faster on acceleration the front gets light and wiggles. That's just you holding on too tight.

As my confidence and understanding of the bike increased the offset we had at the end of the season was almost 10 degrees less than at the start.

Don't judge your speed from mistakes. A slower entry where you aren't tight and making it shake would have worked better than upsetting it and giving yourself a false idea of speed.

Machine set-up and stability help you to stay loose on the bike. The balance is critical: Enough weight on the front to get it turned, but no more.

35

The process of Head Shake begins when the tire hits a ripple and, along with the suspension, compresses. This throws the wheel slightly off-center.

When the suspension and tire release, the wheel is light and flicks back toward a centered position, but again, slightly off-center.

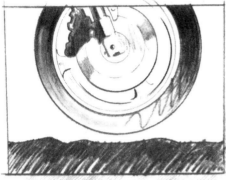 

Still off-center when it loads again from the next ripple; again it is flicked past its centered position.

The cycle of flicking back and forth repeats as the front-end seeks to stabilize through this automatic and *necessary* self correcting process.

Relaxed on the bars allows the front-end shake to remain in the front. Stiffening on them, transfers it, through your body, to the whole bike.

Tight and Wide

Holding too tight onto the bars also makes the bike run wide in turns. Because of this self-correcting, back-and-forth action of the front-end and the outward-bound cornering forces, the bike winds up going wider than it should. Also, the inside bar is the most accessible to hang onto while cornering and if the rider is stiff, he's counter-steering* the bike **to the outside**.

On a fast track you want more fork angle or more offset for stability. Slow tracks: When you steepen head angle you also soften the spring.

Steering Dampers

What about steering dampers? Well, they don't stop head shake completely, but they do limit the travel and intensity of the head shake. Because the damper is mounted very far forward on the bike, it does not have sufficient* leverage* to transfer the shake to the rest of the bike, although some bikes will shake violently if the damper is set too tightly. Taking it one step further, if the steering damper was very long and anchored at the back of the bike, it would transfer the head-shake to the entire bike. The steering damper is not another device to reduce the effects of **SRs**: If you are stiff the bike will shake with or without a steering damper. Dampers are necessary on modern day motorcycles which have steep steering-head* angles, relatively* short wheelbases and lots of power.

When the bike is working right AND you are working right you don't need the steering damper. Mine is at the lowest setting.

Faster Wobbles

Essentially*, the faster you go the more the bike will tend to head-shake, especially coming off the turns when the front really is light and can't follow the road well. You have to ask yourself, "How bad can head-shake get?" If everything is tight and your steering damper is working okay, it only gets as bad as you hold it tight! Remember to relax. Overcoming the "too tight" **SR** is the hard part. Allowing the front to "work" is a standard riding technique which agrees with machine design.

*Here again, too much weight on the front will let the back spin too easy and the bike shakes from spinning and hooking up but usually **you** make it even worse.*

Too tight on the bars is the most common source of motorcycle handling problems.

Bending the elbows and wrists instead of straight arming the bike will set you up to be in a more friendly and relaxed position on the bike. I only vary the grip when I'm making steering changes: Outside of that; my grip is as equal and relaxed as I can make it. Treat the bike like a friend and it won't work against you.

D.G.

Definitions

Areas: Field of study, or a branch of a field of study.

Automatically: Starting, operating, moving, etc. independently.

At-speed: As fast or nearly as fast as you could be or should be going.

Sole: Being the only one; Only.

Inclination: A liking or preference. A disposition or bent, especially of the mind.

Influences: Things with the capacity or power to be a compelling force on another thing or person.

Realize: To grasp or understand clearly.

System: A combination of parts, assemblages, etc. forming a whole.

Flexes: The act of bending.

Contact patch: The actual foot print of the tire where it contacts the road surface.

Track: To follow the course or progress of.

Dazzling: To impress deeply. Brilliant.

Principle: A primary law or truth from which others are derived.

Counter-steering: To guide in an opposing manner or direction. The act of initiating a turn by cocking the handlebars in the opposite direction to the way you wish to go.

Sufficient: Enough to do the job.

Leverage: The mechanical advantage or power gained by using a lever.

Steering-head: The forwardmost section of the frame which holds the bearings, steering stem and triple clamp assembly by which the forks are attached to the bike.

Relatively: Compared to others.

Essentially: Basically.

Notes

CHAPTER 9

Rider Input

The Problem Of Stability

Why do modern sportbikes look the way they do? Is it just cosmetics? Does your machine have design functions you're not using?

By being rigid* on their bikes, riders **CAUSE** handling difficulties. Countless numbers of aftermarket* shocks, forks, steering dampers, custom frames, tire profiles and other paraphernalia* have been designed, manufactured and wrongly purchased by riders to cure self-generated handling woes. (However, a good rider can benefit from using such paraphernalia).

SR #2 Solutions

A number of features have evolved to assist the rider in becoming less of a bad influence on the motorcycle. Some of these solutions are:

High-backed (racing style) seats anchor the rider more firmly, reducing the need to hang on by grabbing the bars tightly.

Large tanks provide elbow or forearm rests during cornering.

Knee slots on the gas tank's side provide a more stable way to hold on, allowing the rider to use the bars less. Tall tanks can also provide a chest rest.

Rearset footpegs give the rider a more stable pivot-point* for moving around and steering the bike.

Similarly, clip-on or lowered handlebars allow the rider to rely less on the bars for a pivot point, drop the rider out of the buffeting* airstream and put the rider in a more favorable* steering position.

SR #2 Effects

Understanding the functions* of the now-common motorcycle design features described above and using them correctly will put you into agreement with your bike.

Wind Riding

Most riders become anxious about being blown around in the wind and tighten on the bars. As the upper body is buffeted by the wind, it acts like a sail*. The bike is then being steered by the wind! Ride loose and low, and the wind's effect on the bike is reduced by at least 75 percent.

Some design features help reduce unwanted bar pressure

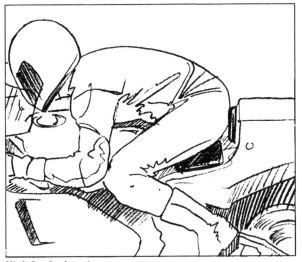

High-backed seats.

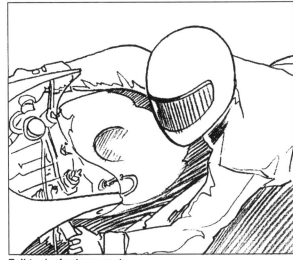

Tall tanks for torso rest.

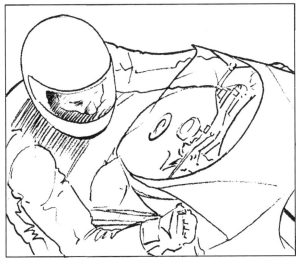

Arms rest on large tank.

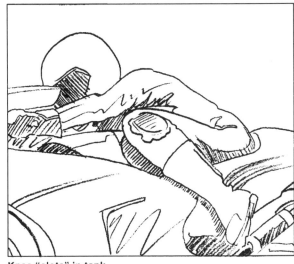

Knee "slots" in tank.

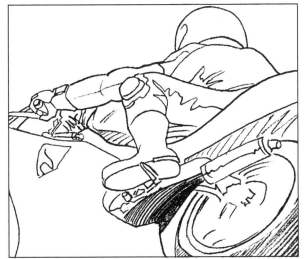

Rear-set style footpegs.

Cruiser style bikes rely on the bars as a primary pivot point.

Auto Throttle

Other key rider jobs are similarly affected. Riding through bumpy turns and being stiff on the bike tends to roll the throttle on and off: the bike bucks even more as you bounce up and down on the seat. Both suspension and traction are affected because standard throttle control is not maintained. This can be quite dramatic. Solution: Use the "**elbow check**" in turns. If you can easily and loosely move your elbows, you aren't too tight on the bars.

Inside Info

Trying to anchor* yourself firmly on the bike requires a place to hold on. Unfortunately, the **inside bar** is the handiest thing to hold on to. The problem created is that the bike will go to the outside of the turn because you are counter-steering (pulling on the inside bar) toward the outside of the turn. Holding onto the bike with one leg or both legs eliminates this often baffling problem. Resting the elbow on the tank can help and having the seat section short enough to use as a pivot point for the body can also be a workable solution.

Fast Turns

In very-high-speed turns the wind is trying to twist you back off the bike, especially if you have a knee out; the knee acts like a sail. Staying as low as possible on the bike helps. Keeping your leg/knee as close to the bike as possible is also good.

Hanging Off

The hanging-off riding style has an unfavorable side-effect in store for riders who don't understand handlebar inputs. Moving up and over from one side of the bike to the other by pulling on the handlebars immediately makes the bike wiggle, especially under acceleration. But pulling yourself back onto the seat by using your outside knee or leg against the tank reduces handlebar inputs and and avoids the problem.

Drive Shakes

The same goes for accelerating out of turns when the front of the bike is light and/or there are ripples in the pavement. The bike shakes because you're holding on tight. Also consider good throttle control; a nice, smooth, even roll-on is very difficult when you have a death grip on the bars.

Wheelie

The very same principle applies to setting a wheelie down. Tight on the bars and wheel not lined up with the bike's direction at set-down produces the shakes.

False Speed

Holding on tight also transfers more engine vibration to your hands and arms. This not only tires them out and makes them numb (which causes you to hold on even tighter) but also gives the impression* you are going even faster than you are and/or that the engine is turning over faster than it is.

False Suspension

Here again, holding on too tight makes the rider receive too much input; the rider senses every movement of the bike when it isn't important. The tighter you hold on, the bigger the bumps seem. Small shakes of the front-end are amplified* as well. **SR** #2 makes them all worse.

Lefts and Rights

The age-old mystery of riders preferring left turns or right turns is easy to resolve*. They're uncomfortable on the bike in one or the other and are simply holding on too rigidly, on their "bad" side.

Blurred Vision

Riding rigidly can shake your helmet and head enough to blur vision. Here again, bumps and wind buffeting are dramatically exaggerated* when riders keep their bodies stiff. The more you try and hold your head still, the more it moves in short, choppy jerks that blur the vision and make your neck sore.

SR #2 Conclusions

Confusion is the result of too much input to the rider at one time. Holding on too tightly could cause up to 11 bad effects in one single turn, possibly even all at once. **SR** #2 creates an exhausting chain-reaction of unwanted input and corrections to the machine.

By being comfortable and having the idea you fit on the bike, your body position will be more conducive to making it easier to control the bike and use good riding technique. In this way you're not fighting yourself. It's most important to use the footpegs to unweight the body while changing positions on the machine. This holds excessive handlebar useage down to a minimum and reduces upper body fatigue.

D.G.

Definitions

Rigid: Not bending; inflexible.

Aftermarket: The market for replacement parts, accessories and equipment for the care or enhancement of the original product after its sale to the customer.

Paraphernalia: Equipment or apparatus used in or necessary for a particular activity.

Pivot: A pin, point or short shaft on the end of which something rests and turns.

Point: A particular spot.

Buffeting: Striking or pushing against repeatedly.

Favorable: Advantageous; giving advantage, opportunity or convenience.

Function: The kind of activity proper to a person or thing. The purpose for which something is designed.

Sail: A piece of canvas or cloth spread to the wind to cause a vessel to move.

Anchor: To secure firmly as if by an anchor.

Impression: A strong effect produced on the intellect, feelings, etc.

Amplified: Made larger or more powerful: Increased.

Resolves: Reaches a solution to: Solves.

Exaggerate: To increase or enlarge abnormally; to magnify.

Notes

CHAPTER 10

Rider Input

Riding and Sliding

Is a motorcycle truly out of control when sliding? How do you save it when the front or rear tire gives up traction? Why don't the fast guys crash when their bikes slide? While wiggles and shakes are distracting, there is a far more dramatic and deadly result from **SR** #2 that you should fully understand and it has to do with sliding.

Perfect Design

Take this idea: A motorcycle in motion is a pretty stable* unit if left alone by the rider. Put the bike into a slide to see if it's true. Does the motorcycle feel stable to you when sliding? It should, if you're doing it right.

When it slides, that first instinct says Chop It but the bike is making a tighter corner from the slide and you don't have to. You stand it up.

In the most typical of slides, you have the back end "coming around." What isn't understood by most riders and something that brings up a very real drawback of **SR** #2, is the fact that the bike actually **compensates* for this slide automatically**.

In a rear end slide the front end turns toward the direction the bike is actually going—into the slide. The main mass of the bike is moving outward and the front wheel turns just the right amount to stabilize it. This feature comes free of charge with every motorcycle. In a car, if the back end comes around, the front wheels turn to the inside of the turn, creating a pivot point for the car's mass, and it spins out. Learning how to drive a car in the snow is mostly a matter of understanding that you have to manually turn the wheel into the skid to stabilize it. You don't on a bike.

If you don't raise it up in a slide, the back end just keeps on coming around.

When the bike slides and **SR** #2 is triggered, the rider with good reactions and a strong back is in trouble. If the rider is successful at holding the bars tight enough that they don't turn into the slide, the bike now acts like the car: The front contact patch becomes a pivot point, except that a motorcycle doesn't spin out, it **highsides**.

More little slides have turned into far worse situations than you would care to know, because of this dramatic result of **SR** #2. I suppose it pays to be slow and weak in this circumstance. In my own experience, having the bike slide and then being stunned* into inaction (an **SR** of a kind), then noticing the bike really didn't do anything wrong (didn't crash), made me understand this self-correcting aspect of motorcycle dynamics. For dirt riders, this is the main tool for cornering.

Many small slides turn into much worse situation from excess rider input.

SR Combination

Chopping the throttle (**SR** #1) and tightening on the bars (**SR** #2) together form a deadly duo. The normal result of chopping the gas when the back slides is immediate traction, which stands the bike up. This is the first stage of a highside crash. If you catch it before the back is too far out, usually it isn't a problem; the bike just shakes a bit as the wheels come back into alignment. If you don't go completely off the gas, the bike is far more stable than if you do!

Front or rear slide and throttle chop will make it stick and launch you over.

Controlled, tire-spinning, acceleration drifts like our heros do on the 500cc GP bikes, would not be possible if they were very tight on the bars or if they chopped the throttle. You have to be able to overcome both of these SRs to do that yourself. (Now we see why 500cc GP guys get paid so much).

You get to appreciate the guys who can keep it sliding, bring it up just the right amount and take it to the paint, on the gas. That's impressive to me and Freddie was the best at it.

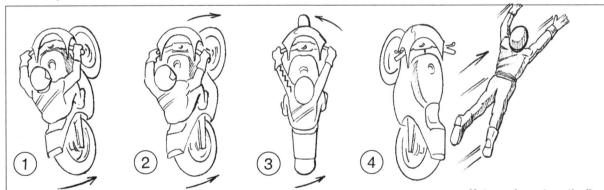

Front Slides

I was watching a race on TV one day and a pro rider I know crashed. As I thought about it, he had been crashing quite a lot recently. In this situation, he got into a turn too hot and the front-end* began to slide, or "push." A pushing front-end "tucks," or turns further toward the inside of the turn than it normally should. The wheel snapped back to "normal" position and then he crashed.

Front-end slides usually occur because too much weight forces the tire past its traction limit. It is possible to have it slide when underweighted; as when accelerating out of a turn with lots of lean angle, but usually the rear gives up first under the acceleration-plus-cornering load.

Motorcycles automatically compensate for rear-end slides by pointing the front wheel into the slide (1 & 2). If the rider tenses up or turns the bars to straighten them, he risks high-siding the bike (3 & 4).

Front-end push isn't as nice and not as common. It happens because the bike's wrong, not set up right, or the tire is wrong.

47

Gas On Solution

The most standard solution for a pushing front is to get on the gas enough to transfer some weight from the front tire to the rear tire. (Remember, the bike's ideal is about 40 percent/60 percent, front/rear). Manually turning the bars one direction or the other causes what I saw on TV (described above) to happen. With a pushing front-end, turning the bars back to a "normal" position is counter-steering, which would make the bike **lean over even more**, which is also what happened. Letting the bike "do its own thing" opens more doors for escaping the above than it closes. Most importantly, the pushing front-end is slowing the bike down at a rapid rate and as it slows the forces are lessened and the bike tends to stand up, get back in alignment, and continue through the turn. That's what you want. **Far, far more front-end and rear-end slides have been "saved" than lost.**

In a very real way you are dangerous to yourself as long as this **SR** can grip you in its claws: But it **can** be overcome. **Take control...Relax.**

It has taken me years to be able to keep from chopping off the throttle when sliding. I hold a steady throttle when a slide starts or even continue to roll into it. Standing the bike up just a little also works to get the bike "hooked-up" smoothly. If you chop off the throttle when the front-end pushes, it will transfer even more weight to the front and then you need a small miracle to save it. Keep your head **and** a steady throttle. Use your knee to hold the thing up if you have to.

D.G.

Definitions

Stable: Resistant to sudden change; steady; reliable.

Compensates: Makes up for or offsets; Acts as a counter-balance.

Stunned: Stupefied, astonished; astounded; amazed.

Front-end: The fork assembly including the front wheel of a motorcycle.

Notes

Rider Input

Man Plus Machine

Hold back from making big changes on the bike until you've had two practice sessions.

Do you believe motorcycles are basically stable or unstable? Are they predictable or unpredictable? What part do you play in this?

Predictable

Don't always blame yourself for errors. Even if you run the same bike, conditions change, suspension doesn't always perform the same. You could be doing it right and the bike needs set-up work.

Just as in a slide, (explained in the previous chapter), your bike can be counted on to act in a predictable* and consistent fashion in virtually* every situation. The rider is the wild card, the unpredictable and variable* component* in the package. And his problem is with the **SRs** that are triggered, nothing else. But, from talking to most riders, you can easily get the false idea that motorcycles aren't predictable at all, that they have an uncountable number of vicious tricks to play on the unwitting* pilot. I'll give you an example.

Every Four Laps

At a national event, one of my private students told me this: "About every four laps the bike shakes violently going through the kink (about a 120-mph turn leading onto the back straight), the front-end comes off the ground (heavy chatter) and I can't figure out what suspension changes to make."

He was very concerned about this and I couldn't blame him so all the possible fixes went through my mind. Finally, the fog of vague* mental pictures, like broken frames and leaking shocks, cleared. "Wait a minute," I said. "Motorcycles don't do anything every four laps. Only riders do. So, loosen up on the bars through the kink; it will stop shaking." It did. In fact, to prove the point, his left clip-on handlebar **broke off** about three laps from the end of the Superbike race and he still wound up fourth and only running 2.5 seconds off the winning pace for the day! You certainly can't hold on too tight with only one handlebar.

Holding On and Traction

When you brake hard, stiff armed, you can get the idea you are braking harder than you are.

Riders have a variety of ways they make this type of thing happen. Basically, all that results is a loss of traction and stability but those two parts of riding are the biggest attention getters (**SR triggers**) there are.

Weight transfers on the bike are an obvious source of traction reduction, as we have seen in the throttle control chapters. But this business of holding on has a huge effect on traction as well. There are a number of ways to minimize this effect, once you understand it. Braking is a good example because most riders go pretty stiff when they get on the brakes and thus transfer more weight onto the front than is needed.

Taking some of the weight of braking-deceleration against the tank lessens the amount of weight on the bars and the result is: (1) You have the rear wheel on the ground (in really heavy braking) a little longer; and (2) in less-than-all-out braking the front end has more travel to work with the pavement ripples, maintaining better stability and traction.

Stiff Corners

After braking, some riders stay stiff-armed on the bars; the upper body is driven forward by a deceleration force of about 0.2 to 0.3 G, leaving extra weight on the front-end of the bike. Potentially, up to 100 pounds of weight is transferred to the front end when that weight could be on the seat or tank, 24 to 36 inches further back. Forgetting to relax is all this really is.

Stiff-armed while braking and in turns can make your job more difficult by transferring extra unwanted weight to the front-end.

Smoother Throttle

Another advantage of relaxing comes when you get back on the gas. If the rider is already relaxed on the bike, there is up to 100 pounds you **don't** have to transfer, front to rear, with the throttle. That makes the transition, from off-the-gas to back-on-the-gas, much smoother, right from the beginning of the throttle action. This totally agrees with machine design and your goal of getting the bike settled to its 40/60 position as soon as possible. **Allow your body to relax immediately after the steering action is completed.** In fact, ideally, you would be loose right when the tires "bite," at the moment you are at full lean angle.

Active Suspension

There is another trick that will keep you from adversely affecting the suspension over rough sections and pavement transitions*. It is a technique borrowed from dirt riding and horse racing. On abrupt* transitions from flat to elevated (like going up onto the banking at Daytona) or vice versa*, lifting off the seat slightly, even while hanging off, makes the legs an active part of the suspension. The rider's weight is carried lower on the bike; and because the rider isn't bouncing up and down on the seat, he avoids creating even more load changes for the suspension and

Try to keep your weight off the seat except on the straights and mid-turn.

eventually* affecting traction. This applies to any rough road surface. Use your legs to hold your weight up; don't overuse the bars to hold your weight up or to hold onto the bike.

Tankslapper Damper

Picking your weight up off the seat if the bike wobbles violently or slides and catches also works to reduce the effect of your body mass being so high on the bike. This allows the bike to correct and stabilize itself much easier. The less of a "whipping back and forth" mass you become, the quicker the bike will stabilize.

Sit Still

Suspension set-up is done for a given amount of weight in a given position, not for a variable amount of weight or weight positioning. All it means is that the bike can't "think" with you moving around on top of it. One of the most obvious things about a GP bike is that you can't move very far forward or backward on the seat.

I ran into a problem with weight transfer a few years back. In an attempt to fully relax on the bike, I took to laying my upper body weight on the tank in turns. It improved the handling in a number of places on the track, especially the slow-to-medium-speed turns. I didn't realize how much moving the weight, which was now transferred to the front, was unloading the rear wheel. When my lap times got good, I unexplainably "lost" the rear end in a fast turn. I experimented with this on other bikes and found the same thing, (without crashing); the back-end gets loose much easier, on most bikes, with your upper body weight on the tank. The bike was set-up fine for my body weight, it just didn't like where I was putting it and I wasn't smart enough to adjust the suspension to my new body positioning.

Weight Transfer

With your feet on the pegs, weight shifts forward or back depending on your upper body's position. 10 to 40 pounds can transfer, off the rear onto the front, just by leaning forward from a straight up sitting position, without even touching the bars. A little more if you rest on them. For the purpose of traction, that is significant.

However, after the clutch is dropped in the classic race type start, with your body over the tank and legs pointed back, no additional weight for antiwheelie ballast is actually on the front-end — **until you get your feet onto the pegs**. Because of acceleration force it's still the most comfortable position; but get the feet up quick.

Sweeper Weight

In fast turns, it is particularly difficult to stay back on the seat because wind drag on your body is trying to tear you off the bike. Most riders find themselves pulling forward on the bike in an attempt to hang on, reducing rear traction to a degree. Staying low on the bike and keeping your knee tucked tight to the bike helps. Adjustments can also be made to the suspension, transferring more weight to the rear if it is a problem. Lowering the rear, raising the front, raising the whole bike and moving the rear wheel forward are four adjustments which will transfer more weight to the rear.

But here again, the basic action of pulling back on the bars can create an adverse effect on the bike, making it shake and run wide in the turn. Not what you want.

Rider Input

Suspension can be adjusted to a variety of road and track conditions. Mismanaged **rider input** creates an unpredictable factor which cannot be adjusted for. By being loose on the bike and allowing it to work, the rider reduces the variables to a bare minimum and allows a workable suspension set-up to be reached.

Also, wrongly having the idea that motorcycles are unpredictable can start a parade of **survival reactions** with the all-too-real and very devastating* result being **doubts** in your own ability.

There is **no way** to counter-steer the bike into a corner efficiently after braking with both arms stiff. Be prepared, be relaxed.

D.G.

Definitions

Predictable: Being what was expected; capable of being foretold.

Virtually: Almost wholly; nearly completely.

Variable: Likely to change, inconstant.

Component: An element or ingredient.

Unwitting: Not knowing or unaware.

Vague: Indistinct; not clearly defined.

Pavement transition: The exact point where one kind of pavement meets another, creating a distinct change in surface as well as occasional bumps.

Abrupt: Unexpectedly sudden.

Vice versa: The reverse order.

Eventually: Finally; at some later time.

Devastating: Laying to waste: Ruining.

C H A P T E R   1 2

Steering

The Forces To Beat

How precise* should your steering be? What are the forces involved in steering a motorcycle? How do you comply* with those dynamics? How quickly should a bike be turned? What actually happens when you turn? What are the limits? How does steering affect throttle control? What are the **SRs** and **SR triggers**? How do they work against you? What are the dos and don'ts of **standard steering.**

Skill Scale

When you can quick-flick you are confident of the settings and the bike.

You can determine any rider's basic skill level by how well he can change directions, steer his bike, flick it in, lean it, get it turned, bend it in, bend it over, crank it over, tilt it over, stuff it in, snap it in—call it what you will, there is a scale of rider ability and nowhere is it more obvious than in this action of riding. Let's review the basics first.

Basic Steering

Everyone tips over (crashes) their bicycle when they first learn to ride. Do you remember? After the training wheels were removed, (if you had them), you crashed. If you never had training wheels, you still crashed. Of course you did; there wasn't anyone around who understood **counter steering** and even if they did, it's hard to communicate it to someone who has never before ridden a single-track, tandem-wheeled (one behind the other) vehicle.

Counter steering: Two magic words. Counter: In an opposing manner or direction. Steering: To guide. It means to guide in an opposing manner. Simple enough. You have the bars in your hands and you're going straight, but you would like the bike to turn, let's say, to the right. "To guide in an opposing manner," you then apply some pressure, at the handlebars, to the left. The bike goes right.

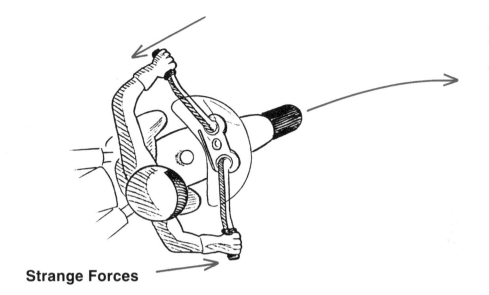

Counter Steering is basic steering technology: Turn it one way and it goes the other.

Strange Forces

Very little in anyone's previous experience could possibly prepare them for that turnaround. Practically everything else in the world works the opposite way; push or turn to the right and it goes to the right, push or turn to the left...

Anytime you are hesitant to turn quick you must fix it so you can just slam the thing.

Two things which might have similarly confused you are the toy-store gyroscope and holding a spinning bicycle wheel by the axle. In each case, your efforts to turn the rotating mass never seem to work predictably in any direction. The force you feel is called **gyroscopic effect. The motorcycle has two very large parts which produce gyro-effect: the front and rear wheels.** Very simply, a gyro is stable when left alone and quite a handful when any attempts are made to change its angle—which is precisely what you must do to steer.

Gyro: The Force To Beat

A motorcycle in motion is a relatively stable vehicle. The faster you go, the more difficult it is to turn because of the gyro effect created by the wheels. That twisting force you feel with either the toy gyro or the bicycle wheel is transmitted back up the fork leg to the frame, where it forces the steering head to one side (tilting the bike).

The closer the contact patch is to the Center of Mass, the quicker and easier the machine will steer.

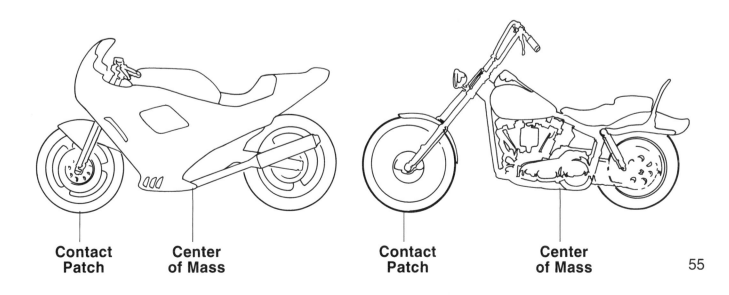

Contact Patch   **Center of Mass**   **Contact Patch**   **Center of Mass**

This is part of the reason that motorcycles with steep steering head angles turn so much quicker than those that don't; the "levers" connected to the gyro force (the fork legs) are at a more efficient angle to tilt the bike over. It's also due in part to the contact patch being that much closer to the center of the bike's mass, making steering the bike easier. The steering head angle is extremely critical to your bike's basic handling characteristics*.

The main advantage in all the high-tech, light weight wheel and brake parts is turning it quicker.

On a 500, when the front is shaking, get it on the back wheel.

The gyro effect, from the rider's perspective*, is simple: When left alone, the bike has some stability; when steering force is applied the bike becomes **potentially unstable** until left alone again. The best example of this is when you encounter a bump while steering your bike: **it will wiggle**. Yet the same bump without the pressure of steering does nothing to the stability.

Steering Affects Throttle

Your mind refuses to let you come into the throttle when you don't know where it's going.

There are quite a number of **SRs** and **SR triggers** attached to this steering business. By simple observation it can be seen that riders don't want to commit themselves with the throttle until they know their steering is completed and that their line will exit on the asphalt, not in the dirt or road barriers. I wholeheartedly agree on this point, but the bike doesn't agree; it wants the gas. This aspect of finishing the steering is why most riders don't get the gas on until two-thirds of the way through the turn. Everyone does this at some time or another, especially on roads they don't know. I don't believe there is any way around this one except to continue to force yourself to crack open the gas and overcome it. But we are talking about steering and it does bring up a very important point about steering: In these situations, the rider is **unable to accurately predict** the final location of his bike, on the road, from the steering he has already done.

Predicting the exact angle your bike will go through the turn, at your Turn-Entry-point, requires skill and gives confidence.

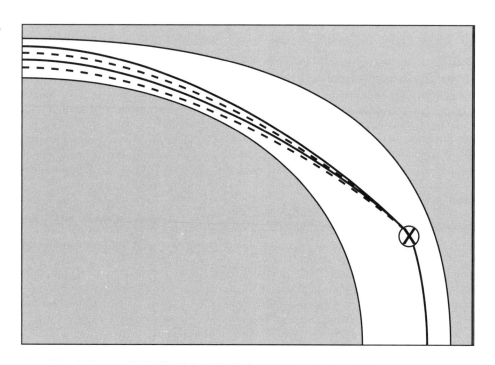

This and other aspects of steering are important. It is very observable that riders begin turning their bikes:

1. Somewhere but not always at the right place.

2. Not always quick enough.

3. Not always to the correct lean angle.

Your final destination in a turn is the result of getting all three correct.

The next five chapters are about how you master the **steering** forces.

While there isn't an ideal or set standard on precision, once you know the basics and know your bike and what you want from it, you can reach your **ideal**. It will be different on a touring bike from a race bike. As an instructor at the Superbike School, I see riders getting stuck, steering for their mid-turn points and forget about the exit of the turns. The apex is just a stepping stone to the exit. Steering is definitely done **for the throttle**. Turn to burn!

D.G.

Definitions

Precise: Exact; definite.

Comply: To act in accord with demands or conditions.

Characteristics: Qualities; distinguishing attributes.

Perspective: A point of view.

Steering

Steer For The Rear

The apex point is where you've accomplished the entry completely and are beginning the exit. It's where you start to concentrate on the rear grip and getting off the turn straight.

You can set it up so it turns easy and then you've got a boat anchor through the middle. You set it up for the least amount of effort through the turn.

A leaned-over bike holds its angle because of the gyro effect from the rear wheel.

There are two gyros, so which one of them does what? Which end actually steers the bike? The front, right? Yes and no.

According to a number of technical reasons, laws of physics* and engineering principles, the following is true: As long as you apply force to the bars, the bike continues to lean further over. However, __once the bike is fully leaned into a corner, the rear end "steers" the machine__. The front-end "turns" the bike or changes lean angle but the moment the motorcycle is leaned over and stable, the main mass of the bike—from steering head back—determines the lean angle it will hold.

The front wheel may hop and shake but it will not deter* the rear from dictating* your lean angle. As already discussed in the Rider Input chapters, tightening on the bars not only adversely affects the handling but is a waste of energy because of this known fact.

If your throttle control is **standard**, the only things that will change the lean angle of the bike to any great degree are a slide/catch action or steering input. The most convincing illustration of this is doing a wheelie coming off a corner. The lean angle of the bike remains the same even though the front wheel has left the ground!

Front-End Duties

Once leaned over in a turn, the front end is no longer steering the bike: It helps stabilize it but does not steer it. But the front end's function is still important. The 30 or 40 percent of the cornering load it is carrying accounts for about that same percentage of cornering speed. In other words, if you added 30 or 40 percent more load on the rear wheel at speed, you would certainly slide it.

The rider's weight lower and to the inside, among other things, helps the bike to turn. Look at the difference in Doug's style in one year of 500cc GP racing.

For steering, you want weight on the front to get that **bite and turn** action. From this perspective, you can get on the gas too early, before the bike has finished getting the extra turning advantage from the loaded front.

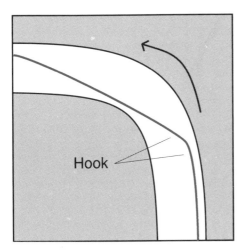

Hook

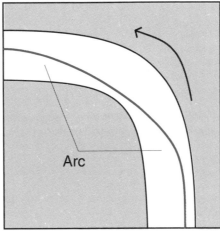

Arc

Weight on the front-end helps the bike "hook" into turns. Getting on the gas too early starts the bike on a constant radius arc before you get it pointed.

False Timing

Turns with a big bump in them can add another interesting twist to this. Turn Seven at Road Atlanta is a prime* example. There is a dip in the middle just by the apex and riders wait to hit it before turning the throttle on. It incorrectly becomes a Point of Timing for them; they think that if the bump makes the bike wiggle with the power off it will make it wiggle even more with the power on. But that's backwards; the front end is working overtime yet 95 percent of all riders wait before doing the one thing that will make it better: Getting on the gas.

Thinking you are at the limit from a bump is going to stop you.

Understanding that the rear of the bike is mainly responsible for stability when the bike is leaned over puts this and many other potentially confusing aspects of riding into perspective. Trying to adjust suspension for the Turn Seven bump would be an enormous waste of time and would be just the kind of thing to stick in a rider's mind because **SRs** make riders gun-shy* of situations that they don't understand. When you begin to anticipate* problems, as above, it just gets worse from there.

Flat or off-camber turns need softer springs so you can keep the same weight transfer front to back.

The gyro effect of the rear wheel controls the stability for most of the bike's mass.

If the front feels like it's riding too high for the back, moving the forks up doesn't always handle it. Here's where the softer spring can help.

Stable Suspension

If you think of the rear (from the steering head back) as the center of stability once the bike is in the turn, it becomes easier to make other suspension decisions. The front needs just enough weight to stabilize itself: Too much makes it feel harsh and too little makes it feel vague with not enough feedback. When the front has just the right amount of weight, it feels planted and follows through with the direction the rear of the bike is giving it. In other words, holding your line.

The bike's going to fight you when you push hard. You are always looking for that limit so you can raise it.

You wind up working harder by reacting to the front-end and bumps it will hit. It's like an SR all on its own: when you anticipate front shakes and stall on the throttle. You can get some help with steering the bike by the slide and catch method but you have to have it turned mostly right to begin with, it's not a technique you use in every turn.

D.G.

Definitions

Physics: The science of matter and energy and of interactions between the two.

Deter: Prevent or discourage from acting.

Dictating: Commanding unconditionally.

Prime: First in excellence or quality.

Gun-shy: Extremely distrustful: Wary.

Anticipate: To feel or know beforehand.

Notes

CHAPTER 14

Steering

The Rules

You don't try to compensate for your error that time in that turn, you wait for the following lap to fix it.

How many times do **you** steer your bike in any one turn? How many times, do you guess, is the right number? **One single steering action per turn**, is correct. That's **rule number one** for steering.

What we call "mid-turn steering corrections," (one or more additional steering inputs) is a **survival reaction** set off by normal **SR triggers**: In too hot, too wide, lost in the turn and so on. In an attempt to correct for their turn-entry errors, riders use steering changes as a catch-all*, cushion or buffer* to handle the uncertainty brought on by the above.

You have to have confidence that the bike will make it through.

Mid-turn steering corrections are generated by survival reactions. And unfortunately, **this rider error**, like all the others generated by **SRs**, goes against the grain of machine technology and good control.

A clean line starts with steering rule number 1: One steering input per turn.

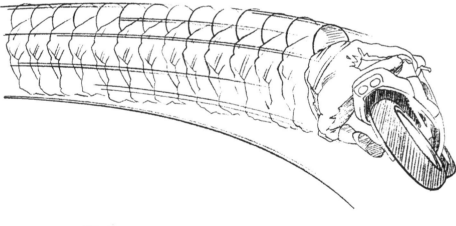

Mid-turn steering corrections can start a chain of rider errors and even result in a slide.

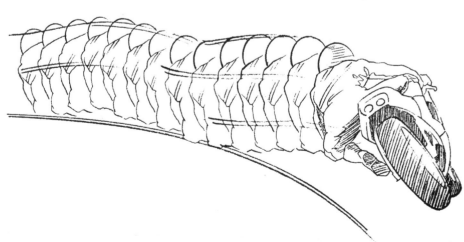

Off/On + Lean

Do you get how this works as an **SR**? The rider sees a situation he doesn't like (going too wide, for instance) and decides to correct it with the steering but, for that moment of **REACTION**, doesn't realize his lean angle will change (become steeper) as a direct result. Believe it or not, this error is as common as throttle off/throttle on.

To compound* the error, a throttle off/throttle on is usually combined with the steering "correction," causing additional, unwanted load changes which affect suspension and traction. Alternately, if the rider has standard throttle control but makes a mid-turn steering "correction," he is coming into the gas AND increasing the lean angle, making the bike less stable and reducing traction. And finally, the steering changes require unwanted rider input mid-turn. It's a mistake in every case. **One steering action is ideal.**

Low-Speed Slides

Over the years, students have come to me or my instructors with stories of sliding our school bikes in one turn or another. Looking at their lap times (typically 15 seconds off the pace), these stories had us scratching our heads in wonder.

The mystery cleared when it was found that, uniformly, these riders were making **mid-turn steering corrections** in combination with **throttle control errors** (off/on), producing jerky little slides through the turns. In most cases, it proceeded to get worse with the rider compounding his errors by (1) straightening the bike to gain stability; (2) going too wide; and (3) then leaning the bike over **even more** in an attempt to avoid running off the track. (In some cases they did run off).

In Over Your Head

You may view this variety of errors in many ways but the bottom line is, you're in over your head if you can't make the turn with one steering input. Why? **One steering movement is the ideal scene for the bike.** Look over some GP videotapes and see how many times Eddie Lawson or Wayne Rainey change lean angle in a turn.

As rules go, there are always exceptions* and this one follows suit. I don't think there is anyone who gets it right all the time. **Small** steering changes in mid-turn are nothing to be ashamed of. Loss of traction and bumps that throw the bike off an intended line will be corrected for by the best of riders. Please realize, though, that these corrections may not even be noticed by the guy directly behind because they are very slight, very subtle* and not quick or jerky.

Realize also that 90 percent of these corrections are unnecessary, that they are truly **SRs** to your current situation. Most riders can figure out that their throttle control errors weren't needed, that they could have left the throttle on instead of going off/on. Likewise, mid-turn steering fix-up jobs are just doing extra work. We've proven it over and over at the Superbike School; with an on-bike video camera looking over the rider's

It's one of the hardest things to feel at ease with, everything is easier than understanding front-end contact and having it stay "underneath you".

shoulder, we have been able to identify up to five steering changes per turn, **none of them needed!** The original steering input would have had the rider wind up in the same place!

Set It and Forget It

The basic rule here is: <u>**Get the steering done with one positive motion and don't put any more attention on it.**</u> There are a number of things more interesting and more important once you're leaned over in a turn. The fewer steering changes per turn, the better. **One steering action per turn is perfect.**

Mid-turn on/offs and readjusting lean-angle come from not knowing the limits of your steering either way — too slow or too fast. You should experiment with quick and slow steering just to get a good feel for the range you can work with. With school students, you can see when they get it right for the first time, not stiff. I know exactly when I'm in over my head. That's when I'm using my knee to keep it from crashing.

D.G.

Definitions

Catch-all: Something that covers a wide variety of items or situations.

Buffer: Any device or material used as a shield or cushion to reduce the danger of interaction between two or more things.

Generated: Started; originated by.

Compound: To increase or add to.

Exceptions: Instances not conforming to the rules.

Subtle: So slight as to be difficult to detect.

Notes

CHAPTER 15

Steering

Lazy Turns and The Turn Scale

There are fearless guys who can just get thru a section quick (steering) but don't know why and they crash.

You spend some amount of time "turning" or steering your bike (going from straight up to leaned over) at every corner. How much time and attention does it cost you to perform this **very important** task? Have you ever noticed how quickly the top guys can do it? Is this just because they have superior equipment?

If how quickly you can turn/steer your bike were on a scale from 1-10, where would you be? If we call this your **steering rate** and Eddie Lawson, Wayne Rainey or Doug Chandler are at 10, where are you? With as much as a 2.0-second **steer rate** being readily observable in most street riders, (Eddie, Doug or Wayne can do it in 0.5-second), I place the average rider at about 3 or 4 on the scale. What does it take to move up the scale and WHY would you want to? What prevents you from steering your bike more quickly?

What is your maximum "Quick Flick" rate? It is one of the key skills of riding.

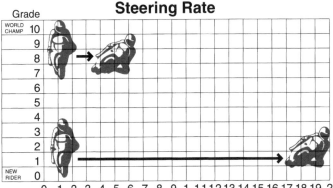

Steering Rate

Grade — WORLD CHAMP 10, 9, 8, 7, 6, 5, 4, 3, 2, 1, NEW RIDER 0

0 .1 .2 .3 .4 .5 .6 .7 .8 .9 1 1.1 1.2 1.3 1.4 1.5 1.6 1.7 1.8 1.9 2
Time in seconds to full lean angle

Steering SR's

Let's face it, steering a motorcycle quickly is scary: You fear it might go out from under you; traction at a quickly achieved, leaned-over position can be doubtful; and, along with the steering process comes lean angle, one of the more classic **SR triggers**. New riders are generally not interested in overwhelming themselves with either **turning too quickly** or **steep lean angles**.

The Lean Angle Credit Card

You don't use a flat deck lean angle very often.

Oddly enough, even though they resist it, street riders in "tense" cornering situations always use far too much lean angle for their speed; so do most racers. This is the **lean angle credit card:** Whether affordable (may safely lean over farther) or not (the frame, pipe, bodywork, or etc. is already dragging on the ground) they crank it over some more! I have repeatedly observed riders dragging parts, when a rider who understood steering and lean could go through the same turn, on the same bike, 5 or 10 mph **faster** and still have leaned-over ground clearance to spare! Is it better to be at steeper lean angles? Would you prefer to be leaned over less and still go as fast?

Most riders lean their bikes over more as a solution to an earlier problem. It's good to have lean-angle credit but not always good to use it.

Error: Too Much Lean

A motorcycle becomes potentially* less stable as lean-angle increases

The steeper you go, the worse it gets. For example, bumps, ripples and slippery stuff are far more likely to cause the bike to wiggle or slide with more lean. And, as we have seen, throttle-control plays a huge part in stability; the steeper you go, the better throttle control must be. Of course, being corner junkies, we love it, right up to the point when the **SRs** are triggered and ruin it. So, let's establish our **goals*** and **purposes*** for this important part of riding and control it.

With extreme lean you are running out of tire or dragging something and lifting them.

The purpose of steering is **to make direction changes. The goal** of steering is **to get through the turn accurately, with as little lean angle as possible** (for the speed you are traveling).

I've noticed I had lean-angle left over and then tried to use it but it didn't help lap times.

Steer Rate, Lean Angle and Speed

Everybody knows that the faster you go, the steeper you have to lean to get around a turn. Right? Okay, I agree. The more speed you have, the more centripetal force is generated "pushing" you to the outside and steering to a steeper lean angle compensates* for that force and allows you to hold your line. But that's not the whole story. To help illustrate this point, let's draw a simple turn and set the speed, turn-point*, maximum lean angle, line and steer rate for the rider. See drawing "A" page 68.

At this speed, using this turn-entry point, and going to this bike's maximum lean-angle, this rider at grade 4 got through the turn fine.

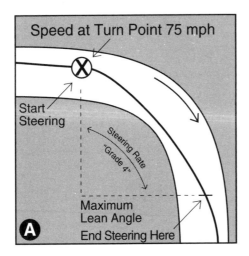

On the next pass through the turn, (Drawing B) our rider becomes lazy and he steers it **a bit slower** but uses the same turn-point, speed, and maximum lean angle. Where will the bike go? **Wide**, of course. (Dotted line)

On the third pass through this turn let's have our rider use the same speed, the same turn point and maximum lean-angle but a **quicker steer rate**. Where will he go now? Too far to the **inside**.

If the rider slows his steer rate he will run wide. (B) If he flicks it quicker he will run too far inside. (C)

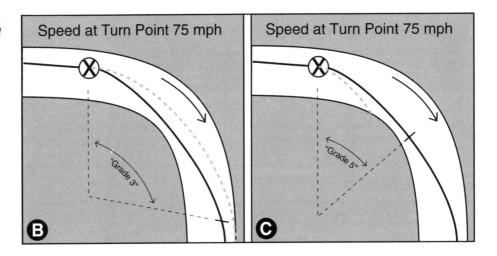

How can he get through this turn (Drawing C) using the **exact same turn-point, line**, and **speed**, but a **quicker steer rate**? What are his options?

Spend less attention on the track surface and more on your riding. Once you have confidence you can get it on your mark every time, you can work on other stuff.

1. A later turn-point might work but would **you** do it if the one **you** had was already working? Chances are you and he wouldn't.

2. Get back on the gas earlier. Maybe, if he can.

3. Get on the gas harder to make it run wider, out onto his original line? It is a possibility.

4. Back in the gas both earlier and harder? Again: maybe.

Doohan is the only one who is getting away with a lot of lean-angle.

5. Use less lean angle? (Drawing D) The lean angle he was using put him into the grass. Why not!

Of all the options, #5 opens more doors than it closes. For example, once you've done it with less lean-angle, it is an easy step deciding to go through it faster next time, using up the leftover ground clearance, still holding your line and staying on the road.

What happens now if the rider wants to **increase his speed** through the turn? If he wants to keep the **same lean-angle** and **turn point**, he will again have to **turn it quicker**.

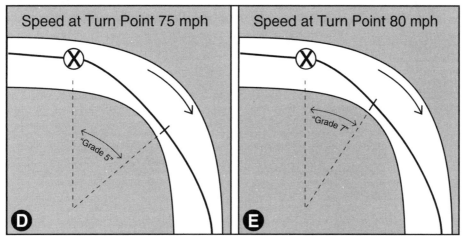

Speed at Turn Point 75 mph

Speed at Turn Point 80 mph

"Grade 5"

"Grade 7"

D

E

Flicking it quicker with less lean angle (D) gets the job done for that speed but if he wants to go faster, he will have to turn it even quicker. (E)

What do we now know? **For a given speed, the quicker you turn your bike, the less lean-angle you use.** Is it desirable to have less lean-angle? **Yes**. Would it give you a safety margin to have more lean-angle available (if needed to get around road or track hazards)? **Yes**. Is the bike more stable at less lean? **Yes**. Could you go faster with the spare clearance? **Yes**. Is traction better with less lean-angle? **Yes**. Does this align with the basic goal of steering? **Yes**. Do you agree with all of this?

In esses, the less angle you use from your quick flick, the less you have to move the bike (side to side) to get through it.

The major important point is how quick, not how far. When I show a school student how you can turn one, that opens the door for them to do it quicker themselves.

D.G.

Definitions

Potentially: Possibly but not yet actually.

Goals: Objectives; things to achieve.

Purposes: Reasons for doing things.

Compensates: Makes up for or offsets; Acts as a counter-balance.

Turn-point: Your exact position or placement on the road, where you start to steer.

CHAPTER 16

Steering

Strange Lines and Quick Turning

Early Turning Errors

Getting an apex figured out keeps you from searching for a comfortable line and keeps you from low entries.

Riders who are lazy with steering **always** compensate for a higher turn-entry speed by beginning to turn the bike earlier than they should. This is a perfect example of **survival reactions #4, #5 and #6** working together. There doesn't seem to be any other choice. It seems like the bike will run wide right away from the higher speed if you don't start turning early and chances are your attention is fixed on the inside of the turn, (the safe, friendly part), and you slowly steer towards it, possibly dragging the brake as well.

Too early an entry creates a decreasing radius turn and opens the door to practically every error in the book: steering, throttle, braking, rider-input and vision. It's a common mistake.

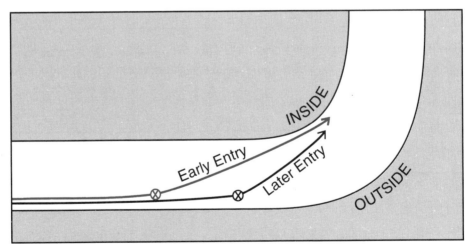

This is the very first, and easiest to observe, error riders make when they begin "trying to go fast." By taking the low line in, the rider is simply trying to buy-off* his **in too fast** trigger. The problem with this **rider error** is that it routinely sets off **SRs #1, #2, #3 and #7** as well!

Low entries keep you leaned too long.

Low lines like this may yield short-term gains in racing where you can pass and block the other rider's throttle drive but in the long run you usually wind up losing mph that would have reduced the time it takes you to reach the next turn.

It's **extra work** because you have to turn the bike at least twice and then sweat out a very hard acceleration through the turn's exit. Besides that, you will wind up with an extra-steep lean angle for at least part of the time. All of these things are attention consuming and provide an open door for mistakes, not to mention the **SRs** that are easily triggered. These are the actual results of lazy steering.

Steering Rule Number Two

What's the rule? <u>**Steer as-quickly-as-possible in every turn.**</u>

The faster the corner the slower you turn it because it will upset the bike.

As-quickly-as-possible means: According to the turn's demands. Obviously, you wouldn't give it a snap-over at 10 mph in a parking lot, because you will fall. On the high end, (say, coming up to a 120-mph turn), you're not going to get it turned that quickly. You won't necessarily fall, but you just can't snap a bike at 120 mph because the gyro effect is too strong. So, the **as-quickly-as-possible** is tailored* to the turn but **it's always A.Q.A.P.**

Rider Quick-Turn Technology

The rider's body action on the bike is a key in making quick-turns. One of the reasons the **hanging off** riding style works so well is that your body is already in a stable position on the bike when you **flick** it in. Part of the technique is to get over into that position well before the actual steering input, usually just before you roll off the gas or pull on the brakes, **early**.

Often times new riders can be observed trying to **hang off** and **steer** the bike at the same moment. **This is a big mistake and only serves to make your bike wiggle at the turn-in point.**

Racer's Advantage

The subject here is how quick you turn and, because of the hang-off technique, the racer has a distinct* advantage. While we know the knee is his lean-angle gauge we must not forget it gives him positive feedback on his quick turn as well, helping to combat **lean-angle SRs**. This **SR** is generated from uncertainty about just two things:

1. How far am I leaned?

2. How far can I lean?

If you always know exactly how far you **can** lean it and how far you **have** leaned it, would you feel more confident about turning quicker? Using your knee as a **lean-angle gauge** answers that question every time you turn. How would your cornering skills look and feel if you could turn it quickly and then spend little or no attention on the lean-angle?

How far you **can** lean (the maximum safe angle) is a question that is answered by experience with your machine, but on any sportbike, your knee can be down way before you've arrived at the maximum safe angle. An experienced racer can find that limit in a few turns by using his knee! Then he's ready to turn quickly.

Turning it too quick will shake the bike or wind you up on the inside.

Using the knee out style helps the racer find his quick flick lean-angle accurately.

When you're "charging" you'll wind up on the bottom because you look in and blow off the turn-point. Back off, get your turn-point and then do it right. The accuracy is more important than the speed. It makes you feel satisfied. Hanging-off is part of the racer's package of techniques. When my toe skid and knee are on the ground, I know that's the limit, I know the wheels will be off the ground if I go any farther.

D.G.

Definitions

Actually: In reality; factually.

Buy-off: Payment or bribe.

Tailored: Adjusted to meet the needs of a particular situation.

Distinct: Unmistakable; clear to the senses.

Notes

CHAPTER 17

Steering

The Key To Speed

What stops **you** from going into turns quicker than **you** do? How many times have you noticed (at mid-turn) that your corner entry speed could have been higher? Exactly what signaled you that your speed was too high coming up to the corner, when it really wasn't? This smells a lot like **SRs**, doesn't it? Let's take up how this relates to steering and how it feels when it goes right.

If you are hesitant, you aren't confident.

Approaching a turn, have you ever felt as though you were going too fast when you were **certain** you could turn the bike? Or, if you are confident you can turn the bike, does your entry speed ever seem too high? (That's the same question posed two ways). All of the 8000 students surveyed immediately said **no**. I say no, too. What do you say? Let's go a step further and ask this: If your ability to turn quicker came way up the scale, could you be confident* going into some turns at speeds that now scare you? Do you get the idea I'm trying to "sell" you something? You're right. I am.

Common* Denominator

Even though they want to, riders have lots of reasons for not going into turns quicker, e.g.*: I didn't know the turn; I thought I would run wide; I would have to lean it over too far; there was traffic in the oncoming lane; and the usual, fear of losing traction as the ultimate* bad result. While each of these seems like a separate, different reason, they all mean you **doubted your ability to get it turned**. The usual response to this doubt is in two parts: (1) Stay on the brakes or off the gas; (2) Steer earlier and slower than intended.

Speed Decision

The Second Rule of Steering—**as quick as possible**—has other uses. Deciding to go faster into a corner must be accompanied by a quicker steering change or you go wide. We know you can use up lots of unnecessary lean angle by lazy turns but here is another, equally important, consideration. **Your quick turn abilities determine your corner entry speed.** Period. End of story.

There are a number of ways to look at this. If you are confident you can turn the bike at your current speed, it doesn't fire up your SRs. If you aren't, it does. Pretty simple. **Solution:** Learn to turn. What happens when you can't turn it any quicker and you've used up all your cornering ground clearance? You are done. That's the limit for you and the bike.

Note: Riding past this limit means losing traction. Many top riders' plans include running into turns fast enough to slide or push* the front tire. That may work in some situations, such as passing, but if waiting for the bike to stop sliding keeps you away from the throttle too long, it can slow you down.

Turning Too Quickly

Can you turn too quickly? Yes. It is possible to steer the bike so quickly that the sudden load on the tires is enough to completely lose traction. That is the real limit. How often does it happen? Well, how many times have you seen someone turn in, lose the front-end and crash (being too heavy on the brakes and turning at the same time not included)? It's **very rare.** On-gas crashes outnumber these 500-to-1. The obvious other exception is turning too quickly on wet or otherwise slippery surfaces. Suspension set too soft, allowing the forks to bottom out, can also promote loss of traction at turn-entry.

I don't think you could ever turn the bike quick enough to lose the front unless it was set up wrong or there was something on the track.

Turning the bike while dragging the brake is delicate work.

Quick-Turn SRs

Whatever your steering skill level, pushing past it is guaranteed to fire-up your **SRs**. In fact, the **SRs** make riders do it **backwards**. The "in too fast" button gets pushed and the rider slows up his steering rate, uncertain of himself and what to do, **when the steering rate should be quickened**. Of course, you can't quicken the steering if you're still hard on the brakes. As mentioned, most pro riders are constantly searching for a speed that pushes (slides) the front-end **slightly**, at turn entry. This gives them a real limit to shoot for **but not to overstep**.

Track Positioning

Some lean-angle changes should not be made quickly. Positioning the bike for a turn-entry with a lazy turn in (to set up for your major steering action) might be looked on as making two steering changes. This would

If you don't have to use full track don't. You can use too much and waste time.

violate the First and Second Rules Of Steering (one steering action/as-quick-as-possible) but it really doesn't. It is **track positioning** and here are some examples of when it is useful:

1. The entrance of the turn is very wide and it would be a waste of time to start your turn from the far outside.

2. A quick, under-acceleration steering change would shake the bike excessively.

3. A slow-turn-in, under-braking turn-entry when positioning the bike quickly for the turn point could overload the front tire and cause the front wheel to lock.

4. A bad bump at the turn-entry must be hit square-on with the bike nearly vertical*; the bike is then quickly turned. Making a quick-turn action or using a steep lean-angle over the bump will bottom the suspension and cause a loss of traction.

It isn't necessary to use the whole road if you don't have to. Position steering is just putting the bike where you want it for the major steering change.

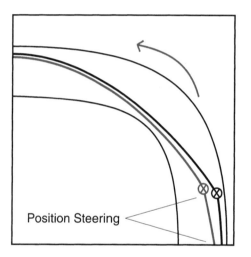

Position Steering

Quick-Turn Remedy

Pushing straight down on the bars has no effect. As you lower your elbows your steering input becomes both more powerful and efficient.

Stiff on the bars under braking and at turn-entry makes turning the bike far more difficult. The most efficient* way to steer is with your forearms as flat as possible, directing your energy into steering and not partially wasting your energy by pushing the bar downward. You instantly "become stronger" (and able to turn it quicker) with every degree of angle you drop your elbows.

Power To Turn

How much pressure can you actually apply to a set of handlebars? Both Eddie Lawson and Freddie Spencer **bent** standard "mustache" bars on late-1970s and early-1980s 1000cc Superbikes! You'd have to see it to believe it, right? Well, something you can see is modern-day frame design which allows riders to turn quicker, without hinge-in-the-middle wobbles.

Modern perimeter* frames basically have two advantages when compared to the frames on the wobble-prone Superbikes of a decade ago. The modern frames:

1. Keep the wheels in alignment when the rider applies steering input.

2. Keep the wheels in alignment when the tires take the cornering load.

The perimeter frame is a very high-tech solution to the **SRs** which used to accompany turning a bike quickly. A quick turn used to wind up the frame like a spring and pay you back in entry wobbles. Quick-turning a big, overloaded touring bike can still give you this 1970s racebike thrill!

Errors

Steering too slowly opens the door for lots of errors:

1. Turning too soon.

2. Going too wide.

3. Waiting too long to get back on the gas.

4. Making mid-turn steering corrections.

5. Using too much lean angle.

6. Going rigid on the bars.

The Limit

The major limit to your turn-entry speed is how quickly you can steer. Improving this one ability will do more for your turn-entry confidence than any other single thing and will help solve all six of the above errors and **SRs**. Can you practice this safely on the street?

Learn to turn.

Confidence in the bike to steer it takes practice. You have to force yourself to get out of the brakes and turn the thing. You have to remember that the act of turning the bike scrubs-off speed all on its own. I see street riders braking and turning at the same time because they don't know this and they always wind up with a low entry speed. They get hit with the **SRs** of going into turns. I think finishing the braking and then relying on your steering is the right way to learn instead of dragging the brakes into turns.

D.G.

Definitions

Confident: Sure of oneself; having no uncertainty.

Common Denominator: A trait or characteristic common to all members of a group.

e.g.: (Latin, exempli gratia); For example or such as.

Ultimate: Greatest in size or significance. Maximum.

Push: When the front end slides.

Vertical: Straight up and down; upright.

Efficient: Acting effectively with a minimum of waste or unnecessary effort.

Perimeter Frame: A frame where the main frame rails run around the outside of the engine from the steering head to the swingarm pivot.

Notes

Notes

Steering

The Three Tools Of Turning

There are three main tools used with steering a motorcycle

1. **How quickly.** (Steer it slowly or flick it quickly; this was covered earlier).

2. **How much.** (As in, lean angle; this was also covered earlier).

3. **Where.** (Your beginning Turn-Point).

All three present the rider with improvement barriers, in the form of mechanical limitations and Survival Reactions.

In the case of Number One, How Quickly, improvement barriers can be illustrated by imagining a street rider trying to lean in a Gold Wing with worn tires and loaded saddlebags. By comparison, Doug Chandler flicking his racebike into a corner makes it look relatively easy. In this case, you're a Leaner (a slow steerer) or a Flicker (a quick steerer), or something in between the two. As usual, **SRs** are the **major** barrier.

It's easy to visualize the mechanical limitations faced in Number Two, How Much: There's no comparison in the attainable lean-angle and available cornering ground-clearance of a Harley chopper vs. a GSXR sportbike; it's obvious from the mid-corner shower of sparks trailing the chopper. And the fear of too steep lean-angle is one of the all-time-classic panic buttons.

Number Three, Where, partly depends on how quickly and how much you can steer your particular bike. You would likely not run your Vulcan 1500 into a very late turn-point and snap it over. And, using an early turn-point is almost completely **SR**-generated and one of the most common cornering errors.

On the open road or track you should choose your Turn-Entry Point. It takes some practice and understanding to see its true value.

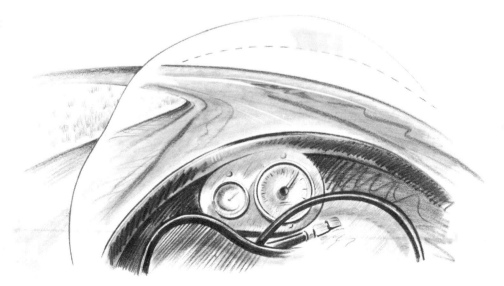

Where To Turn

So, where does a turn begin? Wherever you start to steer the bike. Do you choose a **turn-point** each time you approach a curve? You should. Where do you start to turn if you don't have a **turn-point**? Usually, where your **SRs** force you to!

My turn-point is top priority and everything else is less important as I go around the turn.

A turn-point is the exact position or placement on the road, where you start to steer.

Picking turn-points and using them is an indispensable* tool in combatting general turn-entry panic. And it is probably the most important tool a rider has for accuracy and consistency. Without a selected turn-point, you are leaving it up to the "winds of fate" to determine a turn-entry point. Riders who don't find and use consistent turn-points look ragged on the track; their entries don't look clean and precise, they sometimes make several small steering changes going into a turn and they often hesitate with the gas or go on-and-off the throttle. This is another example of **survival reaction #6:** Ineffective steering.

No turn-point and you will blow the whole corner. You have to keep everything in line and if you error early in the turn you go off line and miss your mid-turn marks.

Major Decision/Indecision

Everyone has a turn-point; whether they consciously selected it or not is the key. **A predetermined turn entry point** is one of the most important **decisions** you make, (if you make it). It's important because so many things depend on that decision. Let's make a list of them:

There are actually eleven important rider decisions that hinge on this simple tool — The Turn Point. (see text)

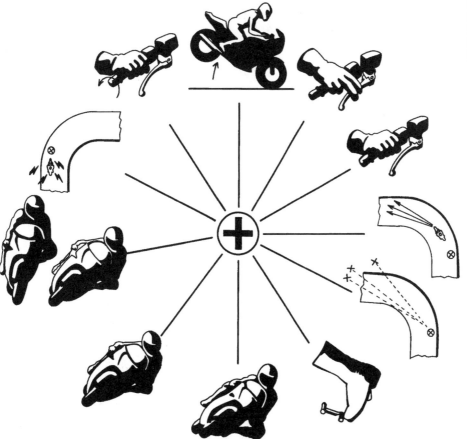

81

1. **How much** speed you can approach the turn with.

2. **Where** the brakes go on.

3. **Where** you will downshift.

4. **Where** the brakes go off.

5. **How quickly or slowly** you will have to steer the bike.

6. **Where** the throttle comes back on.

7. **How quickly or slowly** the throttle maybe applied.

8. **How much** lean angle you will use.

9. **Where** the bike is pointed once fully leaned over.

10. **How many** (if any) steering corrections you will make.

11. **Where** you will finish the turn (how wide you run out at the exit).

*My apex is an imaginary line that splits the corner, entry to exit **and** it's a point you want to run across.*

Please look over this list again. Are these things important? Take a simple thing, like downshifting, and say you waited too late to do it. Would that crowd-up getting off the brake and steering? It could. Does having a **turn-point** give you an exact idea of when downshifting should be completed? I'm not saying this is a major problem for everyone but you may blow the turn by starting a needless chain-reaction of small errors.

Late turn your decreasing radius ones so you can accelerate through the entire thing.

Another prime example of the importance of using your **turn-point as a tool** comes in a decreasing radius turn. A too-early turn-point creates problems with all 11 of the above. Turn-points may vary greatly from rider-to-rider: There is no perfect turn-point for everybody, which only proves that any consciously selected turn-point is better than none at all. We already have a guideline for this: If you can't apply Throttle Rule Number One, the first correction you try should be to change your turn-point.

Correctly adjusting a DR turn is done with your *turn-entry-point tool*. Finding the correct turn-entry-points for a *DR* corner "adjusts" it for good throttle control.

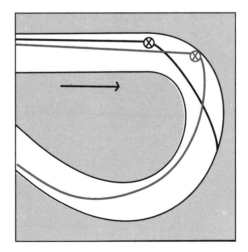

Traffic and Mistakes

Traffic and mistakes may both alter a **turn-point**. Be advised, though, the man who has a consciously selected turn-point knows where he is and the man who doesn't is lost to some degree. **Missing a turn-point gives you immediate knowledge that something else will have to change—before you find it out the hard way.**

Sharpen The Tool

A **turn-point** is a tool and, like any other, requires getting used to. Street riders are faced with these same 11 riding objectives*. The easy flow of normal riding provides excellent practice for finding and using **turn-points**. There is no reason why your riding should not be accurate at all speeds. And, if you can't find turn-points and use them at lower speeds, don't think they'll magically appear when you need them, at high speed.

Anytime you are pushing, you end up over-riding the bike: then you try to compensate by riding even harder. Nine times out of ten it doesn't work.

Go out to the races and observe just how accurate top riders are with **turn-points**. This is one of the most revealing things about the best riders. Whether it is from knowledge or feel, their **turn-points** are extremely accurate, sometimes only varying inches from one lap to the next, throughout an entire race.

Free Attention

All too often, riders try to cover up their basic errors by going quicker, hoping the flow of faster riding will "carry them through." It doesn't, because riding errors are amplified by speed—mostly because of the **SRs** attracted by the danger of going fast, and not choosing a **turn-point** opens the door for all of them.

*You **think** it should be easier if you are going quick but it isn't.*

While it is true you will make and consume far more adrenaline and get all the excitement you can handle by riding without using **turn-points**, lap-time improvement will be difficult. Each of the 11 things listed above carries with it a potential **trigger** for the panic button. Each can consume some, if not all, of **your most valued asset, free** (not captured) **attention**.

Having and using **turn-points** frees up **attention** because you are able to think ahead by simply locating the most important **point of timing** there is. It's not really important whether you have the exact right one or not. **Having the "wrong" turn-point is better than not having one at all.** It will still free up your **attention**.

Observe what the faster guys are using for turn-points.

Every Corner Has A Turn-Point.

How **quick** and how **much** are one thing but not as important as **where**. At the Superbike School we tape turn-points on the track to help students get the feel of using a turn-point. You have to be able to pick your own before you go Banzai in any turn, street or track. By picking a turn-point it gives you an idea of where you are and where you need to be. Attacking corners screws up timing, riding is a flow. If it flows it goes.

D.G.

Definitions

Indispensable: Essential; absolutely necessary.

Objectives: Something worked toward or aspired to; goals.

CHAPTER 19

Steering

Pivot Steering

At how many points do you come into contact with your motorcycle? When steering the bike, which point or points do you use as your **Pivot Point***? If you don't have a solid pivot point, is it harder to steer the bike? Is any pivot point or combination of points better than others? Which ones agree or disagree with machine dynamics*?

There are thirteen different Pivot Points you can use to hold onto the bike. Some work with the machine and some work against it.

❶ Seat Back (1)
❷ Seat Base (1)
❸ Footpegs (2)
❹ Boots to Bodywork (2)
❺ Center of Mass
❻ Knees or Thighs (2)
❼ Stomach or Chest (1)
❽ Forearms (2)
❾ Handlebars (2)

Flick Errors

The **pivot steering** technique is about efficiency. My attention got onto this because of an observed inability in 90 percent of the riders we see at the Superbike School. When asked to demonstrate a quick right-left-right flick like racers use to scrub-in* or warm-up a tire, **they failed**. It's not that the bike didn't go right and left, it's that the rider was **pushing the bike underneath himself**, motocross style—rather than correctly and comfortably moving with it.

On any asphalt-going motorcycle, this defeats both machine dynamics and rider control by using more lean-angle than necessary and making the steering process itself highly inefficient. If you could get around a turn at the same speed with less lean would that be better for you and the bike? Of course it would. The opposite of this push-it-under style is **hanging off**. While in the turn, hanging off delivers exactly what is needed: **less angle for a given speed**. Let's see how you can make it more efficient.

My Discovery

I made an interesting discovery while racing 250cc GP bikes. It corrects the vague* and cumbersome* steering style described above. On the back straight at Road America there is a long, fast, sweeping turn, taken in fifth and sixth gear, where I noticed that bar pressure to turn the bike lasted 3.0 seconds, maybe more. That's two to four times longer than the average steering input on any bike. I also noticed that even though the pavement was somewhat rippled and I was accelerating with steering input, the bike was not showing the normal (under those conditions) tendency to wiggle. I was happy for the no-wiggle handling. On the next lap I noticed a startling thing: I was **using the outside peg as my steering pivot point**.

Mystery solved as to the lack of wiggling. My weight was on the peg, more than 12 inches lower than the usual pivot-point at the tank or seat. How did it get so low?

During the races, I have trouble with the windscreen hitting my helmet. I've broken a few of them this year because I'm up on the pegs and active on the bike.

Weight Redistribution

Using the outside peg as your **pivot point**—while pressure is being applied to the bars, either by just pushing or using a combination push and pull—**reduces your weight on the seat** and puts the majority of your weight on that lower, outside peg. Doesn't putting weight on the outside peg make the bike try to stand up? Not at all: Don't forget the gyro effect from the wheels.

You need to use your feet and be on them.

In fact, since your weight is now closer to the **center-of-mass** for the machine, the bike is much **easier to steer**. Technically, I understand, the bike rotates around the center-of-mass, so the more of the total weight that can be put at or close to the center-of-mass, the better. This is part of the stability factor as well. Your body is not acting like a satellite, far away from that center. The center-of-mass is the part of the bike that moves the least so getting your weight closer to it means you have to move that weight less distance. Your body actually does move but the bike "thinks" it's closer to the center because the peg is weighted, instead of the seat, tank or some other part.

If you fight the bars it will skate the bike.

Pivot Steering starts with the opposite footpeg, moves through the torso and down to the bar. It feels like Power Steering.

Body Strength

Another huge benefit in this is that you are stronger in this position. It's like a camera tripod; the farther out you spread the legs, the more stable it becomes. In this case, the rider is using the farthest point down and away from the handlebars as his pivot-point, with the same result. Using any of the other 13 pivot points on the bike gives you less stability and less strength.

The additional strength comes from the fact that you can now use more of the torso* muscles to help push or pull on the bars. Using any of the other pivot points reduces the number of muscles you can bring into play. Not that you need them all to do the job—**using more muscles just makes it easier**. Any time you steer, it forces a twisting motion through the entire torso. Using more of the torso's muscle groups means it twists less and is therefore a more stable structure.

Push-It-Under Solution

So what about the push-it-under-you problem? **Pivot steering solves it.** When pushing off from the outside peg, you rather automatically go with the bike. Pivot steering answers the reason behind push-it-under-steering as well. In the push-it-under scenario, the rider simply **didn't have a stable pivot point** and was attempting to use his own body mass for stability. Steering the bike in this fashion is like trying to push something away from you while in the water: You have no pivot point, so you move away from the object as much as making it move away from you; which is a great description of the push-it-under style. The push-it-under style also makes riders visibly tense-up different muscles in an attempt to become more stable, and they get more tired as a result. Do you see this?

This is also how you get your short-track or TT bike turned. You set up your short-track bike with a long, low footpeg so you can use it to turn the bike easier.

Steering Advantages

Even if you have your knees firmly clamped on the tank, your legs pressed tightly to the side-panels, your gut and forearms on the tank, your butt up against the seat-back and seat base, both feet solidly on the pegs and a death grip on the bars, you can't get nearly the stability or the power of using **only** the outside peg and pivot steering. Pivot steering puts you in complete harmony with machine design and dynamics and adds a stability to steering you never had before. Take some time working this out: It seems a little strange at first.

Note: Choppers and cruisers, or any other motorcycles with footpegs located far forward of the seat, will not respond to this steering technique. The peg location makes it impossible to use the outside peg as an efficient pivot point.

When and Where

You have to retrain yourself to steer this way. I found that in two street rides, about two-and-a-half hours time, it became "automatically" the way I steered the bike. On the other hand, I tested this out on a street rider who is about a three (on a scale of 1-10) and we rode for 90 minutes, generally working on steering and this as well. He was just beginning to get it right, although still in an awkward way, in about one turn out of 20!

I had trouble understanding why he couldn't do it until I realized that **pivot steering** is actually, for lack of a better term, **double backwards**. Not only is it counter-steering, but pivoted from the opposite side of the bike as well. In addition to this, the fact that you can put so much more power into the bars made him nervous: He was simply afraid to turn the bike that quickly. You really do have to abandon **all** of the "I lean to turn" habits and thinking to make this work.

All The Points

Each of the 13 **pivot points** and their combinations are useful. The undersides of most 500 GPcc riders' sleeves are dirty from contacting the tanks, during and after steering. Often, aluminum parts are shiny from heavy contact with the inside of the rider's boots. Knee and thigh contact points are routinely smudged and the sticky-backed foam padding on racing seats takes abuse from this same process of holding on to the bike both for relaxing on it (as covered before) and for steering (as covered here). Gloves stretch, palms blister, etc., etc. Using **pivot steering** will free you up to use the other pivot points efficiently and correctly.

Use the four major points of contact (hands to push/pull and feet to pivot from). Anything else and you will have trouble with wiggles.

Drill

Before practicing this, first go out and find what pivot points you are **now using**. Then, while mastering **pivot steering**, go back now and then to the **pivot points you were using before** and compare the two results. You might also notice that steering the bike to the right is different than to the left and it's because of the throttle action. You may find yourself both pulling and pushing to go right whereas you'll only need to push for the left-handers. But it doesn't make any difference; this steering technology still works better.

What do you think we should call it? Criss-Cross-Steering? You are going across the body like an X for the pivot/steer action. Center-Steering? You do steer more from the Center-of-Mass of the bike. New Steering? It is a new technique. I call it **pivot steering** because you move from a definite and stable pivot point. But call it what you like, it's the missing link in crisp, efficient, high performance counter-steering, and it works.

To learn this you might start by using something like the seat or your knees as pivot points and graduate up to using the pegs or peg. Just do it a step at a time . This isn't making the bike turn it just makes it more stable while turning it at speed.

D.G.

Definitions

Pivot Point: A place to mount on, attach by or move from; a support, brace or foundation.

Dynamics: How motion and the forces affecting motion are related.

Scrub-in: Roughing up the surface of a new tire by riding on it.

Vague: Indistinct, not clearly defined.

Cumbersome: Clumsy, burdensome.

Center-of-Mass: The point of a body or system of bodies about which all the parts exactly balance each other.

Torso: The human body, excluding the head and limbs.

CHAPTER 20

Vision

Lost In Space, or, Too Fast For What?

There's no such thing as **too fast, too wide, too deep, too hard, too easy, except** when you refer to an **amount of space**. Too fast for the Corkscrew at Laguna Seca would be far too slow for the banking at Daytona. Too slow for the banking (relative to your competition) at Daytona would be unthinkably too fast for the Corkscrew. **Space** does change from track-to-track; but a **rider's view of space** can change from lap-to-lap, in the same turn! It changes from person to person: Aunt Mary thinks **all** curves are frighteningly narrow, at any speed.

SR Space

Following a guy who loses it, you follow him with your eyes to avoid it and forget about what you are doing.

You may regard the **space/area** of a turn as being fixed, unchanging in every aspect* and dimension, but practically* speaking, it isn't true. When for some reason your **attention** becomes (1) narrowed and hunting frantically or (2) fixed on something (Survival Reactions #3 and #4), the door is thrown wide open for every error in the book. And because these **SRs really do happen to people**, the amount of **space** they can **actually** see and use **is reduced**. This is bad.

Instantly reduced awareness of your surroundings is a bad *survival reaction* **which can, at least partially, be overcome with practice.**

While riding, every decision you make is governed by the amount of space you have, think you have, feel you have or believe you have. Look over any riding action you care to and this is true for all. The two basic functions (speed and direction changes) of a motorcycle are totally dependent on the **amount of space** you have to do either of them. Unlike most of the standard riding procedures we have investigated, this one has no mechanical gadgets to assist you.

Fixed Attention

Each of us knows his personal space has, at one time or another, been manipulated by **SRs**. A crack in the pavement, a dark or discolored spot on the road, curbs, manhole covers, white lines, patches, any and all can be a source for concern and **attention capturing** fixation. In motorcycle riding, too much space rarely is a problem: Not enough space, always is a problem. **SRs** connected with space are the worst.

Through the corner if you have some bad spots you tend to look at them and miss the rest of the turn.

All riding survival-reaction-triggers have "not enough space" as their common denominator.

Faulty Design

A real or imagined uncontrollable reduction in space has harm to the body as a **potential** result. **SRs** #3 and #4 are the immediate result. If you were designing **your body**, would you have it staring* at the car which just pulled out in front of it, or would you design it to have a broad view of the road, to find avenues of escape? The "reasoning level" of this type of **survival reaction** is easy to understand, even if faulty: "Keep an eye on things which could harm you."

If I am having trouble, trying too hard or tense, I tend to funnel everything down too tight.

Narrowed or frantically hunting visual awareness = lost = no decisions = no time = full blown Survival Reaction Panic. You may call it an adrenaline rush: We call it rider error.

Ideal See

We've spent nearly an entire book figuring out what the bike wants from its rider and how he can manipulate those design features to get the best possible result. Now we're looking at **what the rider wants from the rider:** How he can **see** enough **space** to stay calm, get his job done and make correct, accurate decisions.

You can get stuck in a rut on how far ahead to look. There isn't any standard to this but usually looking out a little farther helps most riders. Wiley Coyote would not run into so many walls or off so many cliffs if he looked ahead more.

D.G.

Definitions

Vision: The act of sensing with the eyes.

Aspect: Part, feature or phase.

Practically: From a practical point of view; from the standpoint of actual usage.

Staring: To look with a steady, often wide-eyed, gaze.

Notes

Notes

Vision

Reference Points (RPs) Revisited, The Missing Link

The subject of Reference Points (RPs) was apparently* covered to everyone's satisfaction in **TWIST I**. Using RPs on the road or track **works** and graduating up to **wide screen vision**, where you can use all of the RPs and still see the **whole scene** in front of you, is an important, practical and useful tool.

The only thing missing from that technology on "How to See" was a better understanding of **survival reactions**. The discovery that **vision SRs always accompany breaks in "concentration"** gives us a crack to drive a wedge into that barrier.

Sometimes I just go out and watch the other guys ride to get a different perspective on the track and what I'm doing.

Is someone following? At club level racing too much attention is spent on the rider in front. Follow the leader is a common *SR* generated error.

Wide Screen Review

How about a quick review of the **wide screen** vision drill?

Drill One:

1. Pick a spot or an area on the wall or space in front of you to look at. Stare at the area but do it in a relaxed mode, not glaring* intently*.

2. Without moving your eyes, become aware of the whole field of your vision so that each object in front of you can be identified, (a

chair, a lamp, the door, etc.), without looking directly at the individual objects.

3. Still looking at your original spot, move your **awareness** (attention), **not your eyes**, from object-to-object in front of you.

4. That's **wide screen**. Do it some more.

Drill Two:

1. With your eyes, find one object about 45 degrees to the right of your field of vision and one 45 degrees to the left.

2. Shift your focus from object-to-object as fast as you can, getting a sense of how long it takes to do so.

3. Go back to staring at the original spot in front of you (from drill one).

4. This time, move your **attention** (awareness) back-and-forth on the two objects (on your right and left), getting a sense of how long it takes to do so.

Which method, moving your eyes or moving your attention, is the quickest? How much quicker is it? Obviously, flicking your attention/awareness around in your field of vision is far quicker: It moves with the **speed of thought**.

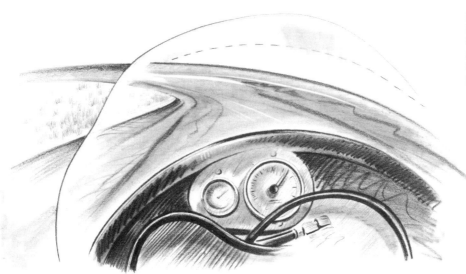

Moving your awareness around in your field of view without moving the eyes gives a broad, continuous visual understanding of your surroundings.

Loss Of Concentration

When we see how well the **wide screen** view works and think of the idea of losing concentration it seems odd because concentration means to focus down on something. That's exactly what we don't want! Do one more experiment for me.

1. Pick four spots in front of you, one a few feet in front and to the right of you, one a bit farther away to the left and two on the wall, one on the right and one on the left, in your normal field of vision, as if you were looking at the road and had four RP's.

2. Move your eyes **as rapidly as possible** from one to the next, stopping as briefly as possible to focus on each before moving to the next.

3. Do this for about 30 seconds.

4. How do you feel?

Almost everyone gets at least some slight feeling of disorientation if not outright dizziness from doing this. **Disorientation** is one of the direct effects of **SRs** #3 and #4. This is the **primary cause of mental fatigue** while riding a motorcycle, especially when riding fast. It is a bad thing.

One more experiment, if you will.

1. Pick the same four spots as above.

2. This time, while moving your eyes from one to the other, keep your field of attention wide, so you can be aware of the rest of the area where you are sitting, while shifting your focus from one point to the other.

3. Is that easier on you?

4. Finally, just to make you feel better, "stare" at your farthest point and shift your awareness, not your eyes, from each one of the four points to the next.

5. Better? It should be. (Give me a call if it isn't).

Controlled View

The ability to get a **wide screen** view is clearly under your control, **when you remember to do it**. If you look around the room now, it is practically impossible to see it any other way but wide. When you ride, this isn't the case. **SRs** close down your view of space when triggered; it's a **reaction to something**. If your chair were suddenly moving at 70 mph through the room, would that trigger **SRs**?

Mechanically speaking, the eye doesn't actually narrow down what can be seen, you simply aren't aware of all you can see when your **attention** is captured or directed elsewhere. **When you remember to do it, the width of your awareness is totally controlled by the mind.** Can you train yourself to remember? Will practice help put you more in control than you are now? I say it can, but you have to decide for yourself, by practice. Is your **attention** wide right now? Could it always be "held out" that wide?

Street Traffic

I'll tell you my secret. I discovered this whole thing one Sunday morning in 1974 while riding to Griffith Park to street race with my friends. I had a vicious tequila hangover. My field of view was about two feet wide and I knew this wasn't going to work; I felt lost on my own street! I suppose out of necessity, my attention popped out wide and I could "see" again; it even made most of my "condition" disappear. From then on, when I left my house, I would usually remember to push my attention out wide. The most amazing thing happened as a result. I **never** again had any trouble in

Your Attention can be distracted by anything. I crashed once because I was on a tighter line getting around a backmarker but had the same speed as last lap. My $10 was on him not the speed.

In faster stuff you can look to the farthest point ahead to judge the distance.

When you do this it opens up your thinking.

traffic with surprise lane changes or sudden critical situations involving four-wheeled motorists. (By the way, I live in Los Angeles). Let me know how it works for you.

This works anytime, driving in your car, anytime. I've been doing it since Keith showed me in 1981 and it has kept me safe as well as fast on the track. Pick a happy medium for your field of vision: not too far or too close.

D.G.

Definitions

Apparently: So it seems; according to appearances.

Glaring: Looking piercingly.

Intently: In an intense or concentrated manner.

Notes

CHAPTER 22

Vision

Wide Screen Control: Different Drills

When you get too "focused" you need a new perspective to improve.

Everyone has experienced what is descriptively* but incorrectly called "tunnel vision" or "target fixation." I say incorrectly because, after all, the "lights" are always on if your eyes are opened but **SRs** distract you from keeping the **wide screen view**. The eye doesn't actually narrow down what is seen, you simply aren't able to see the wide view when your **attention** is captured or directed elsewhere. Is there a difference? **A big one.**

Under Control

Narrowed attention locks you into one particular line and that's trouble.

The difference is whether it is under your control or not: whether it is a totally unchangeable function of the body or if it is adjustable with the mind*. From the drills we've already tried you should be able to see it is controllable **when you remember to do it**.

Take A Walk

A great time to practice "holding out" your attention is while taking a walk. While walking, see how long you can keep your attention out wide. A slightly tougher drill is to walk curbs or railroad tracks, balancing on the curb or track. If you observe someone trying this you will see they begin by looking one or two feet on front of themselves, just like new riders do. My game is to look as far down the curb or rail as possible, keeping the wide screen view and my balance as well. If you run for exercise, do the same basic thing but notice when your attention narrows down, and then, **command it back out**. You may experience some **very** interesting things while doing this.

It May Be Hard

You might notice some resistance while doing these drills. It may make you feel strange at first. You may also experience something pleasant, both mentally and physically. Generally, when you feel good it is easier, and when you don't, it's harder. In fact, it is observable that a person who is feeling good has his attention out wide and one who is feeling poorly doesn't. Is it any wonder that something which was worrying (distracting) a person can be found to exist as a cause for most accidents and mistakes? And, oddly enough, simply widening your **field of attention** can make you feel better.

Just do the drills and you will find it getting easier and you will find new ways to apply it to different situations. You are looking to overcome the **SRs** connected with vision and they're hard ones to beat.

D.G.

Definitions

Descriptively: In a manner that describes or tells the look of a thing.

Mind: That part of a man that reasons and resolves problems.

Notes

CHAPTER 23

Vision

The Two-Step

How much of what you can see on a road surface is really important to you? Is it possible to have too many RP's? What steps can you take to defeat the **SRs** connected to vision and space? How can you tell when you are "over your head"? What is the difference between a point and a reference point?

You don't have to spend that much attention on where you are going if you're looking at the whole track in front of you.

On any road surface, **your attention can hang-up on most anything**. Chewed up or discolored pavement are classic **attention** stickers but rarely affect the bike. In traffic, any car (parked or in motion), pedestrian, surface irregularity, traffic light, intersection, anything there is, can claim your precious $10 worth of **attention**. So why do you look at them? What if you didn't look at them? These are all guaranteed **SR** #3 or #4 **triggers**. And like the other **SRs**, when a rider **becomes aware of fixed attention**, he knows it detracts from his riding.

Everything you notice costs *attention*. **Wide-Screen-Vision makes them less expensive!**

Master Link

It's very easy to link all of the other **SRs** to this one. Throttle changes, steering adjustments, tightening on the bike and braking errors all occur because of some situation that has fixed your attention. You wouldn't go on/off the gas if you were sure of your space. The same is true of mid-turn steering corrections and tensing-up on the bars (to be ready for steering changes): **Without fixed attention, none of them would happen.** Do you agree?

Reduced RPs

Some endurance racers have been known to ride nearly as fast at night as they do during the day. Even with great lights, you can't see most of the things visible during the daytime. I have a similar situation. At Willow Springs, in late afternoon, parts of three key turns (the exit of Turn One, the entrance to Turn Two and the entrance to Turn Nine) become sheets of golden light. To me, it's easier and less distracting* to ride those turns during that time of day simply because you can't see track details.

You've got to get comfortable with the track around you. You sweat in the AM to get good times and then find you can do them effortlessly in the PM.

Am I saying to abandon RP's? **Yes**, when they are just distracting things and not true Reference Points.

The Two-Step

At the Superbike School, we have devised* a method to cheat the problems of **fixed attention going into turns;** we call it the **two-step turn-entry**. At the entrance to every turn we tape marks down on the pavement. (I suppose it seems like an odd idea to put giant marks down on the pavement for the purpose of training riders to quit looking at other marks on the pavement, but it works). The first mark is a **reminder** to look into the turn because 99 percent of all riders leave this important job until far too late. The second mark is the turn-point itself. The **two-step** goes like this:

> 1. You spot your **turn-point** as early as possible. This could be before you brake, while braking, anywhere—as early as possible. (That's one step).

> 2. Just before arriving at your **turn-point** you look into the turn to see where (exactly) the bike should go. (That's the second step).

It's also called the **two-step** because it makes you aware of two major steps, (1) where to turn and (2) where to go afterwards, **before you have done them**.

The two-step is good practice.

The difficult part of this technique is allowing the bike to go straight until you have reached your turn-point. **SRs** are begging you to turn the bike at the same time you look in. This is the "go where you look" **survival reaction, SR #5**. The **two-step** technique helps you defeat it.

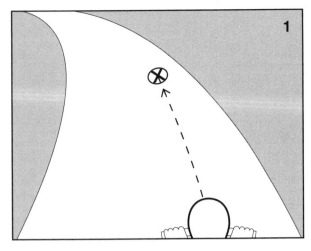

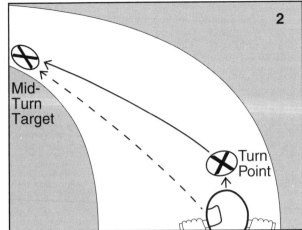

(1) Step one of the *Two Step*: Spot your turn-entry point as early as possible.

(2) Step two: Look into the turn to your mid-turn target a moment *BEFORE* you steer the bike.

Two-Step Solution

The **two-step** solves an enormous number of potential problems. First of all, what would tell you how quickly to turn the bike and how far to lean it over if you didn't already know where you wanted to go? You have to make those decisions **while turning the bike** if you don't do the **two-step**. Practically speaking, that's too late. In other words, the **two-step** gives you all the information you need to produce* accurate steering as quickly as possible.

Knowing where you're going also gives a better picture of the turn and allows you to **set the speed** more accurately for the turn-entry point. This also takes some of the stress* out of braking because it is clearer how much braking is needed and where it is needed. The overbraking **SR** can be linked to this as well. And looking-in early paves the way for getting back into the throttle sooner, starting the whole **throttle control** process at the earliest point.

Using the **two-step** and **wide screen attention** together gives you an ideal scene whereby you can keep track of your turn-point and where you wish to go in the turn, at the same time.

The two-step is a riding technique for handling turn-entry space. The same problems of fixed attention can of course occur mid-turn or in the exit as well as in the entrance. Let's set up a drill to handle the whole turn.

Speed and Space

The throttle is your **space regulator** and contains half the answer. The more you wind it on the less **space** you have to see and act in a given amount of time. At 60 mph you will be 100 yards down the road in about 3.0 seconds; at 120 mph, you're there in half that time.

When you can't see everything that you want to or feel rushed to look at too much with too little time to do it, **you are riding over your head.** Try this:

1. Back-off on the speed for a lap or two, (or on one section of your favorite road), so you can **see** everything you need to see, without

100

feeling rushed or having to "hunt" your way through it. Attention sticking on things is an **SR**.

2. Make the **space** for that turn or section comfortable to be in. **Go only as fast as you can see.**

3. Bring the speed up gradually, using what you can **see** as a gauge of your real skill in that area.

4. When you again notice you are going faster than you can **see**, realize that **you are running into the same barrier at a new, higher level.**

When going quick, I think I'm on the verge of missing my turn-points, but that's just part of going quick.

Looking in early, aligns your vision accurately for the mid-turn and exit.

Goal Of The Drill

The goal of this drill is to find the speed which allows you totally comfortable, wide-screen, smooth-flow tracking of space through the whole turn or section of road. It's not an easy drill but if you persist, the breakthroughs are really rewarding.

Unstick your attention and win.

This helps solve lots of turn entry problems because you are ahead of yourself and helps to keep you from throwing out the anchor going in. Too many RPs is not good; the fewer you have the better. I use my turn-point as an end-of-braking marker as well. Get off the brakes, turn it and get back to the gas; that's where the fun begins. The two-step sets up for doing this with confidence.

D.G.

Definitions

Distracting: Diverting the attention.

Devised: Invented.

Produce: To create by physical or mental effort.

Braking

Nothing New

The average braking distance hasn't changed much in the past 15 years! For streetbikes or racebikes, once the back wheel is off the ground, with 100 percent of the bike's weight being carried by the front wheel, that's the end of the game where braking is concerned: You've run up against the laws of physics. Racers have been able to get the back wheel up, under braking, for two decades!

This is a remarkable statistic when you consider the technical improvements made in the past 15 years. Brake discs are made of carbon fiber; a 900cc streetbike weighs about 150 pounds less; tires are stickier; fork tube diameters are way up and fork flex is way down; frames are stiffer; suspension is much more compliant and much more adjustable; and everything is much more expensive.

Also unchanged is the terror of hard braking. No other control on the bike can produce such dramatic results with so little effort. **SRs** run wild with most riders under heavy braking.

Hard braking is easy: Being controlled and hard takes know how.

Practical Improvements

There have been improvements, including:

1. A more positive feel from the bike; feedback under braking is positive and accurate.

2. Radial tire technology allows for steeper lean angles while braking. So, while the maximum straight-line forces are pretty much the same, the technique of carrying some braking down deeper into the turns entrance has been improved and you find many riders using it.

The lighter wheel parts are a big reason you can carry more brake into the turns than before.

3. Braking over rough pavement is somewhat less likely to lock up the wheel because of all of the above improvements, especially in the areas of weight and suspension. This is an important factor when you consider the fact that most racetracks have pavement ripples caused by racecars; those ripples are usually at the braking points.

4. Brake fade has nearly been eliminated. You can be pretty sure of what you'll have when the lever is squeezed.

Efficient Braking

You're able to structure* your braking from beginning to end in a number of ways, including: Easy at first, gradually applying more lever pressure; hard at first, then easing up; light, then hard, then light again; and all the combinations in between. Which is best?

Trapping yourself into heavy braking at your turn-point is working against the desired result. The basic product (end result) of braking is to get the speed set accurately for the turn. It's difficult to overcome the **SRs** (#7) which compel* most riders to gradually increase the braking force and wind up with too much at the end. There are at least five potential bad results:

1. Turning the bike with too much brake; one of the more common causes of crashes.

2. The turn entry speed is wrong; usually too slow.

3. Too much attention on the braking force; not enough on where you're going and what you're doing.

4. Missed turn-point; puts you off line going in.

5. Too low a turn-entry; gradual instead of decisive turning to avoid **SR** #7 above.

The list could probably also include too much suspension action at the transition from on-the-brakes to off-the-brakes.

Rear Air

Getting the back end off the ground with the brake is, for some odd reason, fun to do. All we're talking about here is **when** it should be off the ground and doing it at the beginning is more difficult for most riders. **Everyone has the feeling they can abuse the front brake whether they have ever locked it up or not.** But there are only two real rules of front brake use and abuse:

1. Don't snap it on too quick. (That bottoms* the front suspension and will allow the wheel to lock).

2. If the front wheel locks up, loosen up on the lever, so the wheel can turn and stabilize the bike. (You lose 100 percent of your steering when the front wheel is locked).

Snapping on the brake lever too quickly is not productive except for photos.

Grabbing it too hard, too quick upsets the bike. Pull it, let it settle, then hard, then light at the end.

If the bike bottoms hard under braking, you need more spring or more compression damping—provided you aren't snapping the brake on but are pulling it as you should, firmly and smoothly. **SRs** go off like fireworks if you lock up the front wheel. The Superbike School has a brake-training bike equipped with outriggers, and it's almost impossible to crash. Yet even on that machine, most riders are tentative with the brakes at first pull.

Rear Brake

I'm going to use the rear if I'm off the track.

It is my recommendation that you master using only the front brake except when riding in slippery conditions. Locking the back brake also puts the bike out of control. The rear wheel, spinning, provides the vast majority of stability for the bike from the steering head back. In other words, everything but the front-end is kept stable by the gyro force of the spinning rear wheel.

People using rear brake hard are scary to me. You can see the shiny spots on their tire where it locked up.

The obvious mathematics of the situation are that the front wheel can do 100 percent of the braking and the back at that point just locks up no matter who you are. Learn to totally rely on the front brake for quick, clean stopping; then, if you still have a use for the rear, go ahead and use it. But realize that the rear brake is the source of a huge number of crashes both on and off the track. I'll leave the final decision up to you. While it is true for most riders that a motorcycle will come to a full stop quicker with both brakes applied, in racing, you don't come to a full stop until you're done.

It's just a waste of time, you spend too much effort getting a little braking from the rear. I don't even put my foot on it except coming into the garage.

In-Turn Brakes

Everyone has used the front brake in a turn before and most bikes have a tendency to stand up when the brakes are applied. While it is true that **you should avoid using the brake once settled into a turn**, there are exceptions (like emergencies) where it is necessary. Crashes often occur when the rider leaves the bike at a steep lean angle or tries to hold it tight in the turn while braking. **Applying the front brake and consciously bringing the bike up at the same time is the correct procedure for emergency in-turn braking.**

Braking after you are in a turn is an error but sometimes necessary. What is the right way to do it?

Brake Magic

There is no real magic in high-tech brakes except **HOW** you use them. Working through the **SRs** that keep you from using the brakes the most efficiently (harder at the beginning) puts you in control. Control with brakes means you have options*. Being stuck with a big handful at the end is the least attractive of all and **SRs** drive you into that scenario.

You can use the brakes to your advantage by braking earlier than someone who goes in really deep because he can go wide and you repass him with a better planned entrance. If you can make a late braking maneuver work by still getting your turn-point that's great. If not, then you are just racing. Some riders go on and off of them while setting up a turn. Braking is a one shot deal, no on/off/on.

D.G.

Definitions

Structure: To give arrangement to. To construct a systematic framework.

Compel: Oblige; to force to a course of action.

Bottoms: Compresses to the limit.

CHAPTER 25

Traction

Pros — Cons and Uses

What do you do with traction? Where can you use it best? How can you abuse* it? How do **SRs** mask your ability to find **traction limits**? What is traction? Does understanding traction make it any easier to find the limits? Does it all just come down to how brave you are?

Your **sense of traction** is an important subject but it can get blown out of proportion; it can even become the cause of mistakes and flawed* riding plans.

A little tire spin helps to get it turned on the exit. Excess tire spin looks great but it is going the wrong way.

How do you like your Traction? Scratch and slide or grip and bite: Your idea of it can affect your style.

New Technology

New tire and suspension technology can cover up and allow riders to "get away with" basic riding errors. Going canyon riding and track racing in the 2000's is an interesting situation for someone who started riding motorcycle in 1957. Old traction memories and standards die hard and I'm not that brave. The 2000's rubber has nearly unbelievable grip in comparison to what I last raced superbikes on in the 1970s but out on the track I see this as a problem for new hot-shot riders coming up and I'm continually amazed at how fast some of them go without a clue as to how and why.

Getting the exit traction right every time is easier and helps with the straights.

Traction Riders

All of the things that arise from this are very interesting. Riders who rely solely on the perception* of maximum traction have a certain style they develop. They appear to be lost if they can't feel that particular band of traction and don't believe they're going fast unless they do feel that traction. Here are some of the results:

*A new approach to the turn could give you a whole new view of traction: just don't try **too** many things at once.*

1. "Feeling" their way into turns, (too slow turn-in rate).

2. Low entries, (start turn-in too early).

3. Mid-turn steering corrections, (slow turn-in makes the final result uncertain until mid-turn).

4. Too much lean angle, (from slow turn-in and from an attempt to get the tire load up so they can "feel" it).

5. Greedy mid-turn throttle application, (to feel the tire bite).

6. Excessive wheelspin at exit, (to keep it loose to know where the traction is—usually, but not always, a plus point).

7. Changing turn points, (their object is not to get the bike turned accurately but to bring the traction to their range).

Easing off – not charging – gets better laptimes. You usually get better entry speeds not charging.

8. Suspension set too stiff, (also, to feel the traction better).

There most probably are additional possible negative results.

Smart Traction

Don't get me wrong, finding the traction limits of the new rubber is an accomplishment. How you find it and then **use** it is our topic. Look at it this way; if maximum tire grip is your **major target** for a turn, it **will** govern how you ride. Any line which gets a **traction rider** to a point where his tires give back this **grunt and bite feeling** against the pavement, will be a good line. But it isn't true, at least not for all turns, and, if it gets out of hand, it can add the above eight errors to the rider's portfolio of techniques.

The hardest part is finding the grip limit going in: the easiest is on the exit.

Try to explore different lines, lean-angles and apexes, not just be stuck on one line.

I remember Wayne Rainey in 1986-1987 spending an enormous amount of his time at the races trying to figure out how to make a fast first lap and it was a battle fought totally with traction. Is it any wonder that he led so many first laps in his World Championship-winning years, 1990-1991-1992? In 1986-1987 he was making all of the above eight errors in

The really hard part is finding the limit every turn, every lap.

search of the traction limits. Is it a crime to make those errors? No, look at what he did with them. The point is that it isn't the only way to go about it: Eddie Lawson did it without the extra excitement.

Traction Terror

The lion's share* of **survival reactions** connected to **traction** are at the **turn-entries**. We know that the very definition of **going in too fast** is "not sure if you can get it turned". And, while running wide in the turn is a concern, possible loss of traction ranks high on the list of **SR** triggers. Is this true for you, too?

Once in the turn, your throttle action controls traction but right at the beginning, **you are essentially at the mercy of the speed you have when the brakes are released.**

Too much entry speed can also foul you up if you go off line because of it.

Crash Statistics

Factually, it's uncommon to go into a turn too fast! Watch racing for 20 or 30 years and tell me what you observe. My eyes tell me **going in too fast** is low on the scale of crash causes. It is rare. Going in with the brakes on too hard and crashing is another thing; that causes crashes fairly often and is an obvious rider error. That most riders misjudge their turn-entry speed, usually on the slow side, is a major stumbling block to clean and quick turn execution.

Brave or Smart?

It may require extraordinary bravery but the most productive use **of maximum traction is right at the turn-entry.** The speed you have at turn-entry is "free" (you don't have to do anything more for it) but any significant speed increases will have to be earned in the hardest and most dangerous ways: with **extra** mid-turn and exit acceleration, the two most common causes of crashing.

Good entry speed makes the mid-turn easier.

My advice? Get a good, solid grounding in standard riding techniques and add the traction limits later. Technique is where most riders are weak and when you combine these two elements, you are hard to beat. Equally important is the fact that good technique allows you to approach the limits of traction and defeat many of the **SRs** connected to it.

Just this year I finally got a good feel for the middle of the turns where I knew what the bike was doing under me.

Traction Defined

Traction: is the **necessary amount of grip needed to get the job done.** You decide if the job is to ride on the traction limit or get through the turn quicker and cleaner. You're winning when you can do both!

You never seem to have enough traction if you are pushing.

Some guys slide the front and some the back, I like to get both ends going and play with traction at the end of the turn. To me that's the most fun but sliding isn't bravery, it's an extension of your skill and ability to control the bike with throttle.

D.G.

Definitions

Abuse: To use wrongly; mis-use.

Flawed: Having a defect.

Perception: To grasp by means of the senses.

Lion's share: The largest part or share.

Notes

CHAPTER 26

Racing

The Tools and Goals

What is the difference between riding and racing? How important a part does your riding skill play in racing? What are the parts of racing?

When it's just you and the track it can be perfect: Other riders add a new set of barriers to the game. You've got all the standard riding techniques to deal with plus the competition's relentless* argument that you don't belong in front of them. **SRs** add yet another dimension* to the game of racing, as do your own goals to succeed and improve.

The Tools

Racing has a number of **tools** you use to accomplish these goals, and each one is a complete subject in itself.

1. Your bike set-up.

2. Your riding skill

3. Your own attitude, or "mental" condition.

4. Your physical condition.

The first, bike set-up, is practically a mystic art for most riders. No matter how adjustable the bike is, finding the correct set-up is often a tedious* trial-and-error procedure even for the best riders. Suspension, gearing and engine combinations these days are practically limitless. This book does not address those subjects.

Racing carries over to street. The high speeds of racing make the street easier. You have more control because you adapted to higher speeds. You don't go into panic mode as easy.

On a 500 I work on getting off the corners better so I can improve the bike, like making rideheight changes, gearing selection, etc.

Suspension adjustability goes up with dollars spent; both factors are practically limitless.

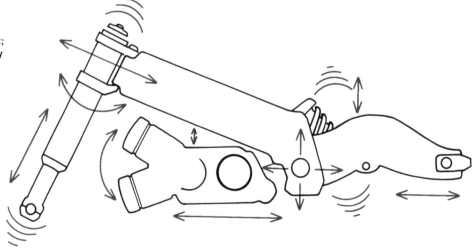

The second, your riding skill, has a number of parts to understand: That's mainly what we're talking about in this book. It often requires great effort to apply what you know to different situations and not become stuck in a riding rut. Every top rider I know has had days when they tried twice as hard and come up with no change in lap times. On the other hand, understanding correct techniques, which agree with machine design and rider requirements, allows you to spot and eliminate riding errors and not confuse them with other problems.

The third, attitude or mental condition, is often the most difficult to adjust. Many riders count on racing to smooth over life's rough edges, at least for the time they are riding, but life's upsets have a way of riding with us. Save for mechanical malfunctions, I have found there to be an actual reason for reduced performance or crashing, which could be uncovered with careful questioning, **in every situation**. That's the downside. The important part is that **mental condition** is your horsepower to push through **SR** barriers and gain **understanding, inspiration** and **efficiency** with your riding skills.

Focused ~~but not too focused~~ is the right way to go racing.

The fourth, your physical condition, must be good enough to do the job of riding; if it's not, your attention can become hopelessly stuck on the manifestations of poor physical condition. Racing is an outward-looking activity and attention on the body drives you inward. Physical conditioning* is often confused with mental conditioning. They do affect each other to a degree. Mainly, a tired body triggers **SRs** which result in mental fatigue. There are thousands of qualified Physical Sports Training professionals who address this.

Good physical condition makes it easier to do consistently. You've got to be good for the duration.

Numerous examples exist, both past and present, of riders strong in one or two areas but lacking in others, who have never quite made it. Yet guys who are just mediocre* in all four have done extremely well. Serious flaws in one will affect all the others. Without getting too complicated, can you grade yourself on each?

Important Parts

The two other main components of racing are not tools but are nevertheless quite important:

1. The competition.

2. The track.

The first of these, the competition, usually has some affect on how hard you try. Traditionally*, lap times come down when the competition is tough and stay the same or slower when it isn't. This is a part of the game which is played both on and off the track. What the competition is doing can either inspire or deflate you to some degree. Riders will instinctively* use anything they see as a weak point against you. A common example of this would be to "show a wheel" to someone in a place where you're a little quicker (but can't really pass), trying to rattle them. Passing in a place where you know the other guy will get you back, but doing it to break his rhythm*, is another **very workable** example.

Everybody wants to get underneath you going in and you have to go off your good lap time marks to protect your inside. Once you break free, then you can put some time on them.

The second of these components, the track, is the playing field. Here again, you are using the tools of racing, mainly riding skill and bike

set-up, to conquer it. While each turn has its own character, **your job** is to correctly reapply the standard riding techniques to each turn. The mental aspect can definitely come into play here. Riders have tracks they like and dislike, types of turns they feel strong in and some they don't feel strong in. Trouble with downhill sections is a complaint I often hear. Bumpy sections are another classic source of trouble. The old saying, "everyone rides the same track," is both the good and the bad news. If you're going faster than the competition, you've figured it out better than those guys; if you aren't, you haven't.

In Competition

If you use someone else for a marker, you're lost. Pay attention to your own riding.

Your riding skill is just one of the four important tools but without a rock-solid plan on how to approach the track, in close competition, you can wind up riding the other guy's race. What is there to be gained by changing your riding to match another's, while dicing for 25th place? Realistically, a competitor in 25th place is making as many or more errors than you are in basic technique. It's fun to beat someone but long-term improvement is more important.

Running valuable laps practicing your own style puts you to work on your problems, not solving someone else's. Stick with **your** plan, it is the one you **can** change.

Don't follow, you'll never pass.

That's Racing

Never make the mistake of thinking someone is holding you up; that's racing, and you're holding yourself up. Never mind that you run up his tailpipe in the middle of every turn and become frustrated; that's racing. You're faster in the turns but he outbrakes you and gets ahead; that's racing. The unfortunate truth is that he is in front and you are blowing it in more places than he—for whatever reason. (In fact, if you run up on someone and have to roll off, that's you blowing the basics of **throttle control**).

I could have had him in another lap.

My tires went off.

Traffic got me.

I know I can beat these guys.

There is another old saying: "The BS stops when the green flag drops." And one of the great joys of racing is the fact that everyone **is** trying their best, no matter what they say. That's racing.

Racing Gauges

There are a number of ways to gauge your skill or improvement:

1. **Who you can beat and where you can beat them.** Home-track guys are hard to beat on their own turf. If both of you go to a new track and you smoke him, that's an interesting statistic. Your skills transfer to other tracks whereas his don't; you are better. Until you're running up front, this is the least important gauge.

2. **Your overall lap time improvement.** From practice-to-practice or race-to-race at the same track you should be improving your lap times. Keep your lap-time sheets in a binder* for accurate comparison.

You'll find lots of improvement at first then it gets harder when you are closer to the quicker times.

3. **How fast others have gone on the type and model of bike you have.** This is especially true if you aren't running up-to-date equipment. Find out how fast others went on what you're running.

4. **Your times compared to the fastest guy or the lap record.** If you start out the season running 10 seconds off the leaders and then cut that gap down a bit each race, that's a good indicator.

5. **Your track section times, both in terms of improvement and measured against someone who is faster.** Cut the track into important sections and get a friend to time you and someone faster in each section. This pinpoints the exact areas to target for improvement and shows you where your efforts are working and where your efforts are not working. Have your timer separate the fast sections from the slow ones whenever possible.

6. **Your practice or qualifying times compared to your race times.** At the top, you rarely see big time differences from one to the other. In the middle and lower skill levels, riders often rely on getting "pumped" for the race to go faster. I suppose you could call that a plan but at which skill level would you like to be riding?

Inspiration

Inspiration comes under the heading of **mental condition**. It is the area of breakthroughs in racing and it really is a tool. Adding a dash of inspiration to go faster is an important part of racing. It takes that very ingredient to push through the **SRs** which fight you, tooth-and-nail, for every single additional increased 0.25-mph, for every half degree of lean angle, for every 1/100th-second earlier on the gas, for every additional ounce of steering input pressure, for every foot of widened attention on the track. **Pushing through survival reactions makes you feel good.** It can be a conscious or an unconscious decision to go faster, turn quicker, slide more and so on.

What does that mean? It means you're winning the internal struggle against the **SRs** and that's guaranteed to improve your spirits. When we talk about it as a tool, that means it should be used only when needed and when appropriate* and not as a cure-all. There are dozens of examples of riders who started off strong, truly **inspired**, but came to a grinding halt in their careers when **inspiration alone** would no longer work.

The Basic Racing Goal

The goal in racing is to beat the other guys. You have to figure out how to go faster than them. There are four tools to use for that purpose and even though your riding skill is the most important one and will bring you the most reward, it can be "overused."

Think about this: Once you have a good understanding of the standard riding techniques, it's time to look toward the other tools for help. Over the long run, new ways to apply the basics will present themselves. But on a particular race day, it's unreal to improve your basic skills enough to matter. At the next lap time "band," these basics will still be sitting there as the main barriers. I can promise you that.

It's not easy to get all the basics under your control. Far from it. Riders who consistently get them right are rare; but you can be beating a dead horse, expecting more from the standard techniques than is available on a single day. Just as being in good physical condition will not improve your suspension or engine, your riding skills cannot improve a sour outlook on the day, a mis-jetted carb or a lack of sleep.

What's the condition of your four tools of racing? How well do they work? Which is your worst? Which is your best? Don't forget your best.

Getting out with other riders gives you firsthand experience with them. It's valuable because you can see what **not** to do. In many cases that can be more important than seeing what **to do**. Your bike **set-up** should be done by experienced people who can get it right and safe. **Riding skill** — You acquire that. After reading this material, you know what the proper techniques are. Now you need some saddle time to perfect them. **Mental condition** — By being prepared and having a plan you can keep it fun and have a good attitude. **Physical** — Basics like good food and cardio-vascular exercise are needed to stay fit. Adequate shape gives you full attention to spend on the race, especially towards the end.

I began racing because I was inspired by one of my idols. You can get a terrific amount of personal satisfaction out of this sport. My personal goal is to perfect my skills against the track (not the public roads); beating the other guys proves I was more skillful than them on that day. Winning a national championship means I had a clearer picture of the season and made intelligent decisions throughout the year.

D.G.

Definitions

Relentless: Unyielding, pitiless.

Dimension: Extension in a given direction.

Tedious: Tiresome or boring due to extreme length or slowness.

Conditioning: Making suitable for a given purpose.

Mediocre: Moderate-to-low in quality: Average.

Traditionally: A time-honored practice. A customary method or manner.

Instinctively: Prompted by instinct, natural; unlearned.

Rhythm: Regular recurrence of elements in a system of motion.

Binder: A notebook cover with rings or clamps for holding paper.

Appropriate: Suitable; fitting.

Appendix

Rider Checklist

1. **Oil at Proper Level**
   A. Engine
   B. Transmission
   C. Chain
   D. Forks

2. **Wheels Are In Line**

3. **Forks Don't Bind**

4. **Chain Adjusted**

5. **Tire Pressures Are Correct**
   A. Cold Pressures Front _____ Rear _____
   B. Hot Pressures Front _____ Rear _____

6. **Steering Head Bearings Tight**

7. **Front Axle Cap Bolts Tight**

8. **Axles Tight**

9. **Wheels Are Balanced**

10. **Controls Are Comfortable and Usable**

11. **Fork Travel Correct**
    (Forks should not bottom out or top out)

12. **Shock Travel Correct**
    (Shocks should not bottom out excessively but should use most of the shock travel.)

13. **Throttle Operates Smoothly**
    (Doesn't stick, no excessive free play.)

14. **Brakes Work Well**
    A. Pads are making good contact on disc.
    B. Pads are not binding disc.
    C. Enough pad material.

15. **Tires Have Enough Rubber**
    A. Unevenly worn or stepped tires can cause handling difficulties.
    B. Old racing tires dry out and become "greasy."
    C. Race tires work best when they have just been scrubbed in and have plenty of rubber.

16. **Enough Fuel**

17. **Master Link in Place**
    (Master link should be safety wired unless it is an endless chain.)

18. **Someone to Record Lap Times**

    Most of these items are not things that a technical inspector looks at. They are items that directly affect your ability to put your equipment to use as a racer. They ensure that you can make it around the track without major mishaps (enough fuel, etc.).

Race Day Record ①

Date _____

Track _____

Racing Organization _____

Length of Track _____

Number of Turns _____

Weather Conditions _____

Ambient Temperature _____

Elevation _____

Classes to be Run _____

Tires Run: Brand _____

Compound/Number _____ Front _____ Rear _____

Tire Pressure: Front—Cold _____ Rear—Cold _____

Front—Hot _____ Rear—Hot _____

Tire Mileage: Front _____ Rear _____

Jetting
Mains _____ Pilot _____ Air Correction _____ Air Screws _____

Needle _____ Slide _____ Float Level _____ Other _____

Gasoline Type _____

Gas/Oil Ratio _____

Ignition Timing _____

Spark Plug Heat Range _____

Cam Timing: Intake _____ Exhaust _____

Valve Adjustment: Intake _____ Exhaust _____

Gearing
Countershaft _____ Rear Sprocket _____ Overall Ratio _____

Shock Dampening
Front—Compression-Rebound _____ Rear—Compression-Rebound _____

Spring Settings
Front— Pre-Load _____ Rear—Pre-Load_____

Lap Times
Practice _____ Races _____

Position Each Lap _____

Points Earned _____

Prize Money Won _____

Comments _____

_____

_____

_____

_____

Rider Checklist

1. **Oil at Proper Level**
   A. Engine
   B. Transmission
   C. Chain
   D. Forks

2. **Wheels Are In Line**

3. **Forks Don't Bind**

4. **Chain Adjusted**

5. **Tire Pressures Are Correct**
   A. Cold Pressures Front _____ Rear _____
   B. Hot Pressures Front _____ Rear _____

6. **Steering Head Bearings Tight**

7. **Front Axle Cap Bolts Tight**

8. **Axles Tight**

9. **Wheels Are Balanced**

10. **Controls Are Comfortable and Usable**

11. **Fork Travel Correct**
    (Forks should not bottom out or top out)

12. **Shock Travel Correct**
    (Shocks should not bottom out excessively but should use most of the shock travel.)

13. **Throttle Operates Smoothly**
    (Doesn't stick, no excessive free play.)

14. **Brakes Work Well**
    A. Pads are making good contact on disc.
    B. Pads are not binding disc.
    C. Enough pad material.

15. **Tires Have Enough Rubber**
    A. Unevenly worn or stepped tires can cause handling difficulties.
    B. Old racing tires dry out and become "greasy."
    C. Race tires work best when they have just been scrubbed in and have plenty of rubber.

16. **Enough Fuel**

17. **Master Link in Place**
    (Master link should be safety wired unless it is an endless chain.)

18. **Someone to Record Lap Times**

    Most of these items are not things that a technical inspector looks at. They are items that directly affect your ability to put your equipment to use as a racer. They ensure that you can make it around the track without major mishaps (enough fuel, etc.).

Race Day Record ②

Date _____

Track _____

Racing Organization _____

Length of Track _____

Number of Turns _____

Weather Conditions _____

Ambient Temperature _____

Elevation _____

Classes to be Run _____

Tires Run: Brand _____

Compound/Number _____ Front _____ Rear _____

Tire Pressure: Front—Cold _____ Rear—Cold _____

Front—Hot _____ Rear—Hot _____

Tire Mileage: Front _____ Rear _____

Jetting
Mains _____ Pilot _____ Air Correction _____ Air Screws _____

Needle _____ Slide _____ Float Level _____ Other _____

Gasoline Type _____

Gas/Oil Ratio _____

Power Commander (Files) Settings _____

Spark Plug Heat Range _____

Cam Timing: Intake _____ Exhaust _____

Valve Adjustment: Intake _____ Exhaust _____

Gearing
Countershaft _____ Rear Sprocket _____ Overall Ratio _____

Shock Dampening
Front—Compression-Rebound _____ Rear—Compression-Rebound _____

Spring Settings
Front— Pre-Load _____ Rear—Pre-Load_____

Lap Times
Practice _____ Races _____

Position Each Lap _____

Points Earned _____

Prize Money Won _____

Comments _____

_____

_____

_____

_____

Rider Checklist

1. **Oil at Proper Level**
   A. Engine
   B. Transmission
   C. Chain
   D. Forks

2. **Wheels Are In Line**

3. **Forks Don't Bind**

4. **Chain Adjusted**

5. **Tire Pressures Are Correct**
   A. Cold Pressures Front _____ Rear _____
   B. Hot Pressures Front _____ Rear _____

6. **Steering Head Bearings Tight**

7. **Front Axle Cap Bolts Tight**

8. **Axles Tight**

9. **Wheels Are Balanced**

10. **Controls Are Comfortable and Usable**

11. **Fork Travel Correct**
    (Forks should not bottom out or top out)

12. **Shock Travel Correct**
    (Shocks should not bottom out excessively but should use most of the shock travel.)

13. **Throttle Operates Smoothly**
    (Doesn't stick, no excessive free play.)

14. **Brakes Work Well**
    A. Pads are making good contact on disc.
    B. Pads are not binding disc.
    C. Enough pad material.

15. **Tires Have Enough Rubber**
    A. Unevenly worn or stepped tires can cause handling difficulties.
    B. Old racing tires dry out and become "greasy."
    C. Race tires work best when they have just been scrubbed in and have plenty of rubber.

16. **Enough Fuel**

17. **Master Link in Place**
    (Master link should be safety wired unless it is an endless chain.)

18. **Someone to Record Lap Times**

    Most of these items are not things that a technical inspector looks at. They are items that directly affect your ability to put your equipment to use as a racer. They ensure that you can make it around the track without major mishaps (enough fuel, etc.).

(Use these and make copies for your notes.)

Race Day Record ③

Date _____

Track _____

Racing Organization _____

Length of Track _____

Number of Turns _____

Weather Conditions _____

Ambient Temperature _____

Elevation _____

Classes to be Run _____

Tires Run: Brand _____

Compound/Number _____ Front _____ Rear _____

Tire Pressure: Front—Cold _____ Rear—Cold _____

Front—Hot _____ Rear—Hot _____

Tire Mileage: Front _____ Rear _____

Jetting
Mains _____ Pilot _____ Air Correction _____ Air Screws _____

Needle _____ Slide _____ Float Level _____ Other _____

Gasoline Type _____

Gas/Oil Ratio _____

Ignition Timing _____

Spark Plug Heat Range _____

Cam Timing: Intake _____ Exhaust _____

Valve Adjustment: Intake _____ Exhaust _____

Gearing
Countershaft _____ Rear Sprocket _____ Overall Ratio _____

Shock Dampening
Front—Compression-Rebound _____ Rear—Compression-Rebound _____

Spring Settings
Front— Pre-Load _____ Rear—Pre-Load _____

Lap Times
Practice _____ Races _____

Position Each Lap _____

Points Earned _____

Prize Money Won _____

Comments _____

_____

_____

_____

_____

NEW

RIDER TRAINING CLASSICS

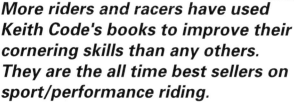

More riders and racers have used Keith Code's books to improve their cornering skills than any others. They are the all time best sellers on sport/performance riding.

Order Today!

NEW *"A Twist of the Wrist"* AUDIO CD, read by Keith with dozens of NEW NOTES and COMMENTS to clarify and add depth to this classic instruction manual. Get it straight from the man in this brand new 4 CD set.

NEW *"The companion video that brought life to Keith's "A Twist of the Wrist" is now available in DVD. Just like the book, the video went on to become the world's best-selling and most widely viewed instructional tape. YOU CAN SEE IT now in all the clarity and convenience of DVD format.*

Keith Code's Books and Video	Cost Each
A Twist of the Wrist, Volume 1 *(115 pgs/89 pictures)*	$19.95
A Twist of the Wrist, Volume 2 *(117 pgs/99 pictures)*	$19.95
The Soft Science of Roadracing Motorcycles *(166/120)*	$19.95
A Twist of the Wrist Video *(107 minutes)*	$24.95
A Twist of the Wrist Audio CD	$27.95
A Twist of the Wrist DVD	$26.95

CALIFORNIA SUPERBIKE SCHOOL, Inc.
Ph: **(323) 224-2734** • Fax: **(323) 227-7877**
e-mail: **cornering@earthlink.net**
website: **www.superbikeschool.com**

Shipping & Handling (per item): $3.95 in the U.S. (excluding Alaska and Hawaii)
$6.95 for others (including non-contiguous U.S.)
CA Residents please add Sales Tax (per item): Books $1.64 / Video $2.05.
Audio CD $2.30 / DVD $2.22

RAINEY'S WAY

After 20 years of racing **WAYNE RAINEY** is at the top. Starting his roadracing career with **KEITH CODE** as his trainer brought both of them to a new understanding of how a racer thinks. That thinking is written down in **"THE SOFT SCIENCE OF ROADRACING MOTORCYCLES."** Wayne says, *"You really can change your ideas and go faster.* Each chapter has questions and drills that will improve your racing. *"I think the guys coming up need to do these steps."* Buy and read **"THE SOFT SCIENCE OF ROADRACING MOTORCYCLES"** today! 120 photos, diagrams and illustrations, 166 pages.

. . . .

"THE SOFT SCIENCE OF ROADRACING MOTORCYCLES"